D1027082

HOW TO COOK WITH
ONIONS, SHALLOTS
LEEKS & GARLIC

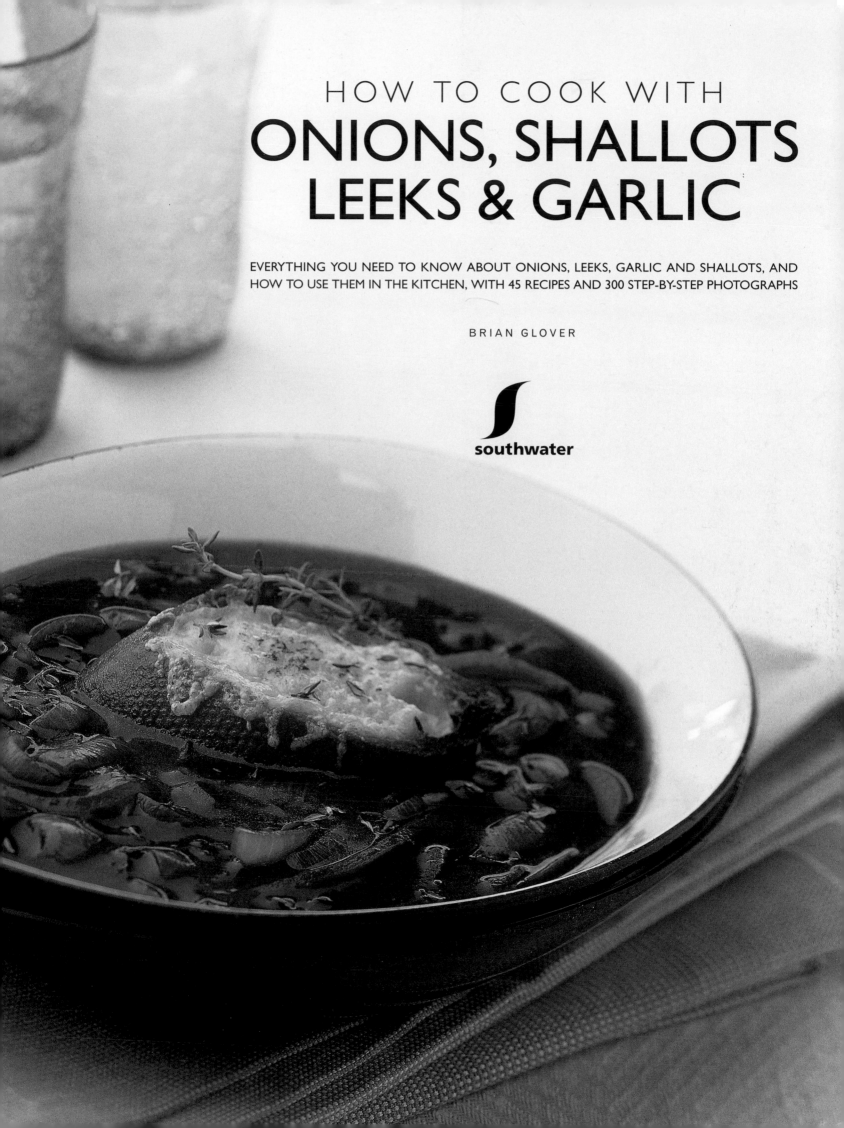

HOW TO COOK WITH
ONIONS, SHALLOTS
LEEKS & GARLIC

EVERYTHING YOU NEED TO KNOW ABOUT ONIONS, LEEKS, GARLIC AND SHALLOTS, AND
HOW TO USE THEM IN THE KITCHEN, WITH 45 RECIPES AND 300 STEP-BY-STEP PHOTOGRAPHS

BRIAN GLOVER

southwater

This edition is published by Southwater, an imprint of Anness Publishing Ltd, Hermes House, 88–89 Blackfriars Road, London SE1 8HA; tel. 020 7401 2077; fax 020 7633 9499

www.southwaterbooks.com; www.annesspublishing.com

If you like the images in this book and would like to investigate using them for publishing, promotions or advertising, please visit our website www.practicalpictures.com for more information.

UK distributor: Book Trade Services; tel. 0116 2759086; fax 0116 2759090; uksales@booktradeservices.com; exportsales@booktradeservices.com
North American distributor: National Book Network; tel. 301 459 3366; fax 301 429 5746; www.nbnbooks.com
Australian distributor: Pan Macmillan Australia; tel. 1300 135 113; fax 1300 135 103; customer.service@macmillan.com.au
New Zealand distributor: David Bateman Ltd; tel. (09) 415 7664; fax (09) 415 8892

Publisher: Joanna Lorenz
Managing Editor: Linda Fraser
Project Editor: Jennifer Schofield

Designer: Isobel Gillan
Photographer: William Lingwood
Production Controller: Christine Ni

ETHICAL TRADING POLICY
Because of our ongoing ecological investment programme, you, as our customer, can have the pleasure and reassurance of knowing that a tree is being cultivated on your behalf to naturally replace the materials used to make the book you are holding. For further information about this scheme, go to www.annesspublishing.com/trees

A CIP catalogue record for this book is available from the British Library.

Previously published as *Know Your Onions*

Main front cover image shows Baked Stuffed Onions with Tomato Sauce – for recipe, see pages 74–5.

NOTES
Bracketed terms are intended for American readers.
For all recipes, quantities are given in both metric and imperial measures and, where appropriate, in standard cups and spoons. Follow one set of measures, but not a mixture, because they are not interchangeable.
Standard spoon and cup measures are level. 1 tsp = 5ml, 1 tbsp = 15ml, 1 cup = 250ml/8fl oz.
Australian standard tablespoons are 20ml. Australian readers should use 3 tsp in place of 1 tbsp for measuring small quantities.
American pints are 16fl oz/2 cups. American readers should use 20fl oz/2.5 cups in place of 1 pint when measuring liquids.
Electric oven temperatures in this book are for conventional ovens. When using a fan oven, the temperature will probably need to be reduced by about 10–20°C/20–40°F. Since ovens vary, you should check with your manufacturer's instruction book for guidance.
Medium (US large) eggs are used unless otherwise stated.

PUBLISHER'S NOTE
Although the advice and information in this book are believed to be accurate and true at the time of going to press, neither the authors nor the publisher can accept any legal responsibility or liability for any errors or omissions that may have been made nor for any inaccuracies nor for any loss, harm or injury that comes about from following instructions or advice in this book.

CONTENTS

INTRODUCTION

Members of the onion family have been cultivated ever since people started to form communities and grow their own food. Wild onions were gathered and eaten even before that. With a few exceptions, onions are now used in the cooking of almost every culture across the world. There is no country where this indispensable vegetable, in one form or another, is not now grown.

The evolution of the first, wild onions into the cultivated plants that we know today is not entirely clear. Many varieties, such as the common or garden onion, only seem to exist in their cultivated form and are not known to grow wild at all. There is a "missing link" in the development between the wild species of the plant and today's cultivated onions.

The mystery surrounding this transition suggests that the cultivation of onions occurred a very long time ago. People would seem to have perceived onions as good things to eat very early on in history, and onions are among the first plants to have been grown to add flavour to the human diet.

Onions belong to the allium family, which contains more than 300 species. Many of these different varieties are grówn in gardens, some as ornamentals in flower borders, others as herbs and edible plants in vegetable patches. For a long time, botanists disagreed about whether the alliums belonged to the larger plant group of lilies (*Liliaceae*) or amaryllis (*Amaryllidaceae*), but now most place them in an order all of their own – the *Alliaceae*.

From the grower's point of view, alliums are very easy to identify. They form bulbs, or fleshy leaf bases; they have long, narrow, flat or tubular leaves, usually blue-green in colour; they have round, globular heads of flowers made up of many individual flowers; and all, to one degree or another, have the same unmistakably characteristic onion smell, especially when the bulb or leaves are damaged or broken.

pejorative associations have been made. They are forbidden to certain social groups and are sometimes considered taboo or to have evil powers. The effect of their odour on the breath and sweat has led them to be labelled as vulgar, and unacceptable in polite society.

The relationship of the onion family to people throughout history is marked by these contradictory attitudes. While onions and other alliums are revered and praised and popular in dishes around the world, they are also frowned upon and rejected by many cultures and social groups.

Left: Alliums are an important crop in France as its traditional cookery has always made very good use of these vegetables, especially onions and garlic.

The pungent onion smell is caused by the presence of allicins – chemicals that include volatile compounds of sulphur – which are released by the action of enzymes when any part of the plant is cut or bruised. It is these compounds that make the eyes water when an allium is chopped and which give onions that are used in cooking their characteristic flavour and bite.

The alliums' inescapable chemical signature has brought them to people's attention from the earliest times. Their smell and taste have made them into plants with an ancient and special place in the evolution of human culture.

From the earliest records, it appears that onions have always been regarded as important foodstuffs and imbued with symbolic and religious meaning: they were grown in the best fields and can be found in important tombs and paintings. However, along with this reverence and value, a number of

Opposite: Onions have been cultivated for thousands of years. Their distinctive blue-green leaves and round flower heads make them easy to recognize.

Right: Delicately flavoured bunching onions and green onions are popular in Vietnamese cooking, and can always be found in their food markets.

ONIONS AND OTHER ALLIUMS THROUGHOUT HISTORY

Whether praised or criticized, the onion family has attracted attention from the very earliest times. In different societies and at different periods in history, these vegetables have been bestowed with symbolic and spiritual meanings and have been considered vital in herbalistic and shamanistic medicine. The onion figures prominently in folklore, literature and even painting: few other vegetable families have such a value-laden history.

The actual origins of the onion are not known. However, they do seem to have been among the first families of plants to have been cultivated and selected. The recorded evidence suggests that onions were first cultivated over 5,000 years ago, around 3000 BC, in Asia Minor – the area of central Asia that now includes modern-day countries such as Iran, Pakistan and Afghanistan. These onions

would have been close relatives of the cultivated varieties that we are familiar with today.

Garlic probably began in this area too, and was then taken to Greece and on to Egypt. A type of garlic (*Allium sativum*) still grows wild in some parts of the Mediterranean, particularly on the island of Sicily. Shallots are also likely to have originated in central Asia and, according to food historian Alan Davidson, were known and used in India before they travelled to the Middle East.

Onions were also being cultivated in parts of China around 3000 BC. These would have been bunching onions (varieties of *Allium fistulosum*), rather than bulb onions. The Chinese also grew leeks, although these were a different variety from European leeks and derived from *Allium ramosum*.

At some point in the Han dynasty, dating 206 BC–AD 221, bulb onions (*Allium cepa*) and true garlic (*Allium sativa*) were introduced into China, probably from India. The bulb onion is still known as *hu-t'sung* or "foreign onion" in Chinese.

The cultivation of onions and garlic is mentioned in some of the early Vedic writings of ancient India. They are also noted in scribal records from Sumer (*c.*2400 BC), which record that the city governor's onions and cucumbers were grown in "the gods' best fields". The mentioning of the various alliums in these early texts shows that they were considered to be a most important crop.

Below: Onions and garlic have been an essential cooking ingredient in many countries, such as Brazil, for centuries.

ALLIUMS IN ANCIENT EGYPT

By the time of the ancient Egyptians, there is evidence that onions, garlic and leeks were being grown and consumed in huge quantities. Onions figure prominently in the decoration and hieroglyphics of one of the Egyptians' best-known legacies – the pyramids. They appear on the walls of the pyramids of Unas (*c.*2423 BC) and Pepi II (*c.*2200 BC) and onions were found in the eye sockets of the mummy of Rameses IV, who died in 1160 BC.

The Greek historian Herodotus, in 450 BC, reporting on his travels in Egypt, writes of inscriptions on the walls of the pyramids that show a breakdown

Below: Egyptian labourers working on the pyramids received rations of onions, garlic, leeks and beer. It was believed that all the alliums provided physical strength and prevented disease.

of the cost of building these great monuments. Among the items listed is an entry showing how much was spent on "black radish, red onions and garlic" for the labourers on the pyramid at Giza.

Centuries later, the 17th-century diarist John Evelyn remarks in his *Acetaria* (1699) on "How this noble bulb was deified in Egypt ... and that whilst they were building the pyramids, there was spent on this root ninety tun of gold among the workmen". When the labourers' onion and garlic ration was cut, they are believed to have gone on strike.

Right: Onions have been found in eye sockets, armpits and body cavities of ancient Egyptian mummies, which were stored in decorative cases. This may have been because onions acted as antiseptics or because they were believed to have supernatural powers.

Above and above right: Onions are commonly depicted in the wall paintings in Egyptian tombs. It is thought they acted both as symbols of eternal life and as food and medicine for the journey into the afterlife.

The significance of alliums to the ancient Egyptians seems to have been very complex. Onions were placed in tombs as food for the journey into the next life and as symbols of eternity because of the circle-within-a-circle structure of the bulb. Many paintings show onions as part of religious symbolism. They were also known as powerful antibiotics and antiseptics. Labourers were fed on onions, leeks and garlic, as these vegetables were believed to keep them fit and well for their manual work.

There is evidence also that the lingering smell of the onion in the body had great significance for the ancient Egyptians. The passage of the onion smell through the body was considered a sign of good health and fertility in women; although it was taboo for certain priests to eat or smell of onions.

The onion family was also popular with the Egyptians' neighbours, the Hebrews. In the Bible in Numbers XI:5, the Israelites led out into the desert by Moses complain about how hungry they are, and remember "the cucumbers, and the melons, and the leeks, and the onions and the garlic", which they used to enjoy in their captivity in Egypt.

The association of alliums with this part of the eastern Mediterranean remained strong for many centuries. For instance, in many European countries, the name for shallots (*Allium cepa*, Aggregatum Group) is derived from the ancient Palestinian port of Ascalon. This was reflected in their old Latin name (*Allium ascalonicum*) given by the Romans. No doubt Ascalon was the place from which shallots were first imported to Rome, and the name stuck.

Centuries later, the tree onion (*Allium cepa*, Proliferum Group), and the shallot-related potato onion, were still both called Egyptian onions by the English and French.

Below: Onions and other alliums are mentioned several times in the Bible. The most famous occasion is when the Israelites recall the pleasures of eating onions, leeks and garlic before their flight from Egypt (Numbers XI:5).

ALLIUMS IN GREEK AND ROMAN TIMES

The classical Greeks used alliums too. Hippocrates (*c*.400 BC), who is credited with founding modern medicine, notes that onions, garlic and leeks were grown in kitchen gardens or harvested from the wild. The food historian Alan Davidson points out that a section of market in Athens was called simply *ta skoroda*, meaning "the garlic", suggesting that the trade in alliums was an important feature of everyday Athenian life. The alliums even merit mention in Homer's great epic poem, the *Odyssey*.

Like the Egyptian pyramid builders, the Greeks believed in the onion's ability to promote health, virility and potency. Onions were used to prepare athletes for games, and competitors not only ate onions, but also rubbed onion juice over their bodies. Greek soldiers were fed on onions to develop a martial vigour, and it was said that the enemy always knew when the Greek army was advancing by the powerful smell of onions that preceded the arrival of the troops.

In Rome, bread and onions were the standard diet of the poor. Archaeologists excavating Pompeii have found onion-shaped cavities where onions were growing in gardens, just as the writer Pliny the Elder (AD 23–79) described in his *Historia Naturalis*.

Because onions played such a vital role in the diet of the poor in Rome, they were held in some contempt by sections of the wealthy elite. The priestesses of Cybele, for instance, refused entrance to their temple in Rome to anyone who smelt of garlic. The poet Horace considered the smell of garlic a mark of real vulgarity and called it "more poisonous than hemlock", and Juvenal mockingly writes of onions as "kitchen gods".

Leeks seem to have been universally popular at all levels of Roman society, which may well have been because they were milder and tainted the breath less. There are many leek recipes in Apicius' 1st-century *De Re Coquinaria*, a cook book intended for the literate middle classes. Apicius was a shadowy figure, and there may have been more than one person known as Apicius involved in the book over a considerable period of time. The recipes show a great love of leeks and, to a lesser extent, onions in a range of sophisticated dishes that include Beets with Leeks in Raisin Sauce,

Below: As with the Greeks, the Roman army was fed on onions and garlic, and took them on their invasions. They are credited with introducing garlic, onions and leeks to Britain, Germany and Gaul.

Above: The Roman emperor Nero was nicknamed porrophagus or "leek eater" because he ate so many of them in his belief that they helped his singing voice and oratory.

Peppercorn Leek Sauce and Quinces Stewed with Leeks. *De Re Coquinaria* contains few recipes for garlic, however, which suggests that garlic was less popular with middle-class Romans.

The Romans not only cultivated and cooked with alliums, but are thought to have been instrumental in taking these vegetables into all parts of Europe.

While Romans enjoyed eating onions and other alliums, they did not imbue them with the same significance as the ancient Egyptians and the Roman satirist Juvenal (*c*.AD 60–140) mocks the Egyptians' contradictory beliefs:

*How Egypt has grown mad
   with superstition
She makes gods of demons as
   is well known
It is a deadly sin to eat an onion
But every clove of garlic has a
   holy power.
A pious country, and with fine
   houses
But every garden is overrun
   with gods.*

ALLIUMS IN THE MIDDLE AGES

After the Romans' introduction of edible alliums to other parts of Europe, these vegetables soon became established as an important part of the European diet. They were popular in the Middle Ages, especially among the poor. Even before the introduction of cultivated varieties, it is certain that wild alliums, such as rocambole (*Allium scordoprasum*) and ramsons (*Allium ursinum*), would have been gathered and eaten. The English words leek and garlic come from the Anglo-Saxon word *leac*, meaning plant, and *garleac*, meaning spear-shaped plant. In Anglo-Saxon, the leek was known as *porleac* and the onion *ynioleac*. Onions get their name from the Latin *unio* via the French *oignon* and Anglo-Norman *union*.

Alliums became an important crop in medieval Britain, particularly leeks, which were one of the few vegetables to withstand a normal winter unprotected. In the *Forme of Cury* (*c*.1390), a cook book written for Richard II, a *salat* was made from *persel, sawge, grene garlec, chibolles* [Welsh onions], *oynouns and leek* all dressed with oil and vinegar. And *porray* (from *porrum*, the Latin for leek) was a white soup made from leeks, almonds and rice.

The trade in alliums was important in medieval Europe. Onions from Brittany and garlic from Picardy are recorded as having been sold in London food markets as early as the 13th century.

By Chaucer's time, in the late 14th century, it is obvious that leeks were considered commonplace, everyday fare. He often uses the phrase "Not worth a leke" to suggest something that is entirely worthless.

Because they were so hardy, leeks could be grown in the coldest places and are associated particularly with Scotland and Wales, becoming, in Wales, a symbol for Celtic doughtiness and survival. Legend has it that the Welsh wore leeks, like feathers, in their caps, as a badge of identification during their victory over the Saxons in AD 640. It is probable that these would have been wild alliums – ramsons or rocamboles maybe – rather than the familiar modern-day leeks. But by Shakespeare's time, the Welsh wearing of leeks on their national day – St David's Day, March 1 – had clearly become well established. In the play *Henry V*, Pistol taunts Fluellen about his Welshness by promising to knock "his leek about his pate upon Saint Davy's day".

To this day, leeks still figure as a part of Welsh identity. They are an essential ingredient in cawl, a comforting soup or stew of lamb and leeks, which may be considered traditional Welsh soul food. Championship leek growing is still a major competitive hobby in many areas

Left: In medieval herbals and medicinal manuscripts, many members of the onion family were recognized to have curative and therapeutic properties.

Left: In Chaucer's The Canterbury Tales *the Summoner's vulgar character is shown by his love of garlic, onions and leeks.*

The ribald and lewd associations of onions and leeks started early in Britain. This Anglo-Saxon riddle dates from before the Norman conquest of 1066:

*I stand erect and tall, well-rooted
I stand proud in bed
I am hairy below. Sometimes the
    fair peasant's daughter ...
... grips my body and holds me
    hard ...
I will bring tears to her eyes.*

Above: An illustration of garlic from Pierre Jean François Turpin's Flore Médicale *showing the bulb structure.*

of south Wales. Most people, however, have taken to wearing the less odorous daffodil on St David's Day.

Although onions were important in dietary and medicinal terms in medieval Europe, the Roman inhibitions and prejudices about how onions smell and the effect they have on an individual's moral character also prevailed.

Throughout the Middle Ages, alliums were associated with vulgarity. For the Egyptians and Greeks, the alliums were thought to promote strength, fertility and vigour, and it was only a short step until onions became associated, in ribald terms, with licentiousness and sexual prowess. In the 14th century, Chaucer's lecherous Summoner in *The Canterbury Tales* is described thus:

*Wel loved he garleek, onions, and
    eek lekes,
And for to drinken strong wyun, reed
    as blood.*

Similarly, in William Langland's *Piers the Plowman*, an allegorical poem dating from the 14th century, Gluttony is offered "a pound of garleek" as an inducement to step into the ale-house rather than go to church.

In France, the various members of the onion family were also associated with sexual potency. King Henry IV, for instance, was commonly reputed to have been baptized with garlic water, so prodigious was his sexual potency and so strong his breath.

Within late-medieval philosophy, edible bulbs, such as garlic and onions, were considered among the least noble of food plants. Existence was structured into a Great Chain of Being, a hierarchy which placed God at the top and inanimate objects, such as plants, at the bottom. All creation was ascribed a level in this hierarchical way of seeing the world and bulbs were placed at the very bottom.

THE ALLIUMS' FALL FROM GRACE

Despite their associations with the poor, vulgar and lecherous, onions, garlic and leeks continued to be popular in British cooking until the 17th century. Eating them uncooked, however, began to be frowned upon and was seen as a distinct social taboo, particularly for women and those who held social pretensions or aspirations.

Towards the end of the 17th century, there was a noticeable rise in the social prohibition against garlic, the most odorous of the alliums. The diarist John Evelyn, a great grower and eater of vegetables, wrote a treatise on salads as a preface to his *Acetaria* in 1699. Regarding "garlick" he writes: "we absolutely forbid it entrance into our salleting, by reason of its intolerable rankness, and that made it so detested of old … to be sure it is not for ladies' palates, nor those who court them".

Below: In some sections of society onions were considered as only fit for poor people as in this scene of humble living called Preparations for Lunch *by Bernard Lepicie.*

Above: Towards the end of the 17th century, alliums became unpopular in genteel society and tended to be associated with the poor and vulgar. Although onions were still used in cooking, they were rarely used as a main ingredient in their own right.

Throughout the following centuries, garlic features little in British cook books, and although onions continue to appear in countless dishes, they rarely figure as a main ingredient in their own right. In Hannah Glasse's *The Art of Cookery Made Plain & Easy* (1747) onions are pickled, stewed, "ragoo'd with cucumbers" and made into a pie. Garlic, however, is not included. Leeks are not mentioned at all by Glasse. As with onions and garlic, they had become associated purely with peasant food and thought unsuitable for the middle classes (at which audience most 18th- and 19th-century cook books were aimed). Isabella Beeton, the great

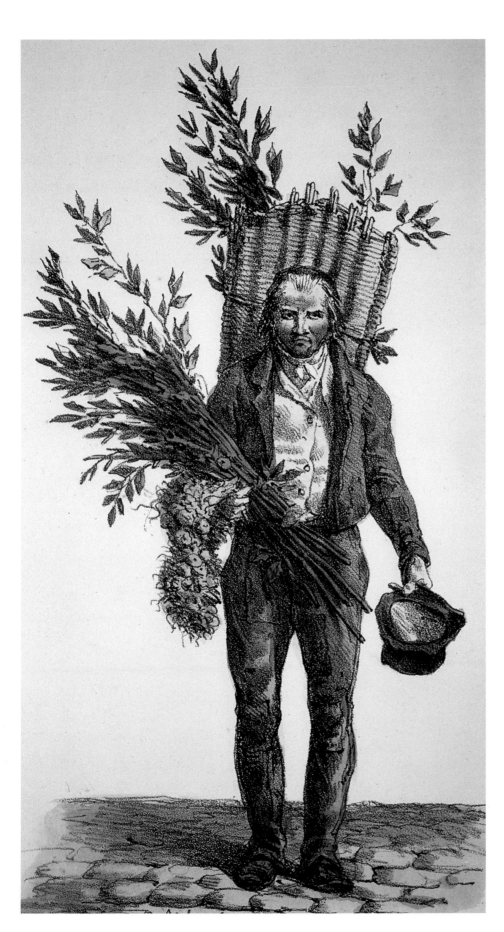

bastion of the 19th-century middle-class kitchen, sums up the doubtful regard in which leeks were held when she advocates boiling them really well or else "they will taint the breath".

Throughout Anglo-Saxon Europe and much of the United States, the social taboo surrounding the effect of onions and garlic on human breath and sweat lasted for almost three hundred years. Undoubtedly, onions, leeks and, to a lesser extent, garlic were still eaten, but to smell of them was considered socially impolite and a mark of low breeding. In countries outside Europe and the United States, similar social taboos were attached to the eating of onions and other alliums. For example, in Japan, to smell of onions or garlic has traditionally been perceived as being discourteous and has a great social stigma attached to it. Japan is still the one country in Asia that makes very little use of garlic in its cooking.

From the time of the earliest records, onions, and in particular garlic, have been accused of exciting sexual and libidinous desires: Egyptian priests were denied garlic precisely because they had to remain celibate. To this day Kashmiri Brahmans and Jains are forbidden from eating strong-tasting foods, in particular onions and garlic, because they are thought to heat the blood and have the ability to inflame carnal desire. Some Chinese Buddhists avoid the prohibited "five strong-smelling vegetables" for the same reasons.

The Hindu sacred texts place great emphasis on the idea that a man is what he eats and rules are given for the right foods. The three upper castes, Brahmans, Kshatryas and Vaisyas, should avoid onions and garlic in their diet. The Sanskrit poem, *Mahabharata,* suggests that onions and garlic should not be eaten by "honourable people".

Left: Garlic became very unpopular in countries such as Britain towards the end of the 17th century, but garlic and bay sellers such as this one were still able to eke out a living in France where garlic was not frowned upon to such a great extent.

THE REHABILITATION OF ALLIUMS

Some countries in northern Europe maintained their antipathy towards onions and garlic, but much depended on the general food culture of a society. In the 1580s, when the German ambassador of the Holy Roman Emperor visited the court of the Byzantine emperor Nicephoros II, his entourage was appalled by the food and the smell of garlic on the emperor's breath. For the northern Europeans, the great consumption of large quantities of vegetables, including onions and garlic, was little short of scandalous. In large parts of northern Europe, especially in comparatively rich countries such as Britain, Germany and the Netherlands, good food was synonymous with meat.

However, many cultures, typically those around the Mediterranean, never fell out of love with the onion family. It was for this reason that the vegetable-loving cultures of the Mediterranean region were for centuries looked down upon as gastronomically uncivilized.

In France, in particular, onions, garlic, leeks and shallots – in fact the whole allium tribe – remained extremely popular at almost every level of society. Brittany, a region well known in the 20th century for its bicycling onion sellers, and the west of France were particularly linked with cooking with onions and garlic.

The French trade in onions and garlic began early; onions from Brittany were exported to London as early as the 13th century. The trade continued until well into the 20th century, with onion sellers cycling around southern English towns selling their familiar strings of onions and garlic from their bicycles. Food writer Lindsay Bareham notes that the last of these onion sellers was still working in the mid-1990s.

Onions and garlic were, and still are, an intrinsic part of much French provincial and peasant cooking. Garlic festivals, such as the garlic and basil fair at Tours on St Anne's Day, July 26, occur throughout France, usually when the new season's crop has been harvested. Even when the alliums were at their most unpopular in Britain, in the 18th and 19th centuries, onions were still celebrated in France. As food historian John Ayto points out, the classic sauce, *sauce soubise*, was named after an 18th-century French general and courtier Charles de Rohan, Prince de Soubise, showing that aristocracy did not see any shame in being associated with onions.

In sophisticated Paris, onions had their ups and downs, but by the early 19th century they were actually thought quite *de rigueur* in polite society. The poet Shelley, writing of a trip to Paris, seems quite delightedly shocked at the

Above: In the early 19th century, Parisian society considered onions and garlic positively fashionable.

thought of the onions' fashionable status: "What do you think? Young women of rank eat – you will never guess what – garlick!"

In Spain, too, onions were consumed with gusto despite the fact that certain elements of society frowned upon the practice. An old Andalusian saying states that "*Olla sin cebolla, es baile sin tamborin* [a stew without onion is like a dance without music]". In Cataluña they celebrate the new crop of their local, large green spring onions (scallions) –

Onions in the United States

Columbus, and then the first pilgrims, took onions and garlic to North America, while the Spanish introduced them to Central and South America. But many varieties of wild onion, leek and garlic grew indigenously in North America and were used by native Americans in cooking and, especially, in medicine. Chicago was named after the Illinois Indian name for "the place which smells of onions". *Chicagoua* – the plant that gave Chicago its name – was probably a form of wild garlic or ramps (*Allium tricoccum*). This species and other wild onions, such as *Allium cernuum* and *Allium canadense,* still grow profusely throughout North America. Père Marquette, the French Jesuit explorer and missionary, who camped on the shores of Lake Michigan in 1670, wrote of being saved from starvation by eating the various kinds of wild onion and garlic that grew there. Later generations of Americans took these plants to their heart, and much onion breeding took place in the first decades of the 20th century. The emphasis was on producing sweet, early-summer-cropping onions, which have a high water and sugar content. There was also a move towards producing low-sulphur and hence less smelly onions.

calçots – with a special feast called *la calçotada*. It consists of green onions, grilled (broiled) over charcoal and served with salsa romesco, made from chillies, nuts and garlic.

Despite the popularity of alliums in such countries, these odorous vegetables were slow to return to favour in England. Onions, shallots, even leeks, but most especially garlic, remained fairly unpopular and became associated with "foreign food". Writing in 1861, in her hugely influential *Book of Household Management*, Isabella Beeton observes rather sniffily of garlic: "It was in greater repute with our ancestors than it is with ourselves ... on the Continent, especially in Italy, it is much used, and the French consider it is an essential in many made dishes". Mrs Beeton gives only one dish that includes garlic – a Bengali recipe for hot mango chutney – highlighting the influence of Indian cooking on the English kitchen.

Why did the alliums stay so popular in some cultures but attract such great opprobrium in others? One answer may lie in the nature of cooking in different cultures. In northern Europe, especially England, and in North America, regional, peasant and rural cooking lost ground

Above: During World War II when onions were in short supply in Britain, leeks became even more important.

in the face of a growing move towards industrialization as people migrated to big cities in search of work. Alliums have always been associated with regional, peasant cooking. These traditions remained strong in all the Mediterranean countries and had a great influence on the middle-class cooking of the day. In Britain, cooking was effectively cut off from its rural and peasant roots and a "genteel" style of middle-class cooking – ironically influenced by notions of French *haute cuisine* – was adopted in its place.

By the late 20th century, the health benefits of the vegetable-based Mediterranean diet, including lots of onions and other alliums, was vaunted in Britain and the United States as a much healthier way of eating. This had always been the case in poorer areas of Europe, where onions have always remained a vital and much celebrated way of injecting flavour into the diet.

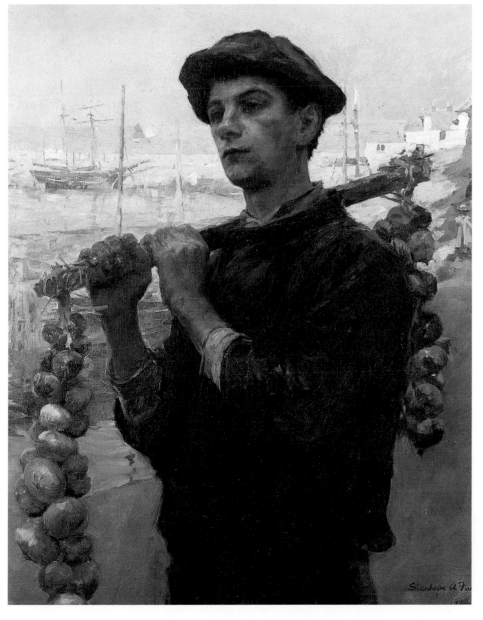

Left: French onion sellers, like this one depicted by Stanhope Alexander Forbes, were once a common sight in many English towns.

ALLIUMS OVER THE LAST HUNDRED YEARS

Apart from long-standing religious and social taboos, the history of the onion family over the last century or so has been one of gradual rehabilitation. In the United States and Australia, the massive influx of immigrants from garlic-loving cultures (Greek, Italian, Hispanic), has had an effect. In Britain, the growing love affair with Indian "curries", especially after World War II, was important, too.

Italian and Greek food, both heavily garlic- and onion-reliant, came into great vogue in the 1960s. Food writer Elizabeth David, whose books on

Mediterranean and French cooking were published in the 1950s and '60s, had a huge impact on breaking down the social taboo against garlic.

There had been a few earlier voices. *The Gentle Art of Cookery* (1925), written by Miss Olga Hartley and Mrs C. F. Leyel, included a whole section solely on onions, including soups, stuffed onions and a recipe for an Alsatian *gâteau aux oignons*. Mrs Leyel was the founder of Culpeper's herbalist shops, head of the Society of Herbalists, and was obviously an adventurous cook and traveller. She includes garlic as one of the essential ingredients in her "Alchemist's

Storecupboard". In 1933, the cookery writer Ambrose Heath wrote his *Book of the Onion*: a whole book (albeit small) devoted to recipes containing onions as a major ingredient. But these were lonely voices.

As the century progressed, the old middle-class sanction against using (and hence smelling of) onions and garlic started to falter. By the 1960s

Below: Onions and bicycles have long been associated with each other because of the traditional French onion and garlic sellers who, even today, can be seen selling their produce.

onion-smelling breath or body odour became less of a problem than it may have been in previous centuries.

Nowadays, onions, garlic and leeks are celebrated as never before. Garlic and onion festivals are held in places as distant as the Isle of Wight in England, and Gilroy, California in the United States. New varieties of onion are constantly being developed and bred, providing a year-round supply. Some restaurants devote themselves to wholly garlic-based menus, introducing such unusual dishes as garlic ice cream. Thousands of websites on all members of the onion family have been launched.

Exciting discoveries are being made about the medicinal qualities of the alliums. Today, the onion family is perhaps more popular and considered more indispensable than at any other time in its long and complex history.

Above: Specialist growers selling many different kinds of garlic, shallots and onions are a familiar feature of French and Italian markets.

Right: These enormously long strings of garlic for sale at Korla market in the Kinjiang Province in China demonstrate the popularity and importance of this allium in Chinese cooking.

and '70s, using garlic in food became a mark of culinary sophistication and trendiness. The famous "garlic dinner", cooked by American chef Alice Waters in 1976 in her Berkeley restaurant Chez Panisse, launched a huge garlic revival in mainstream American food culture and was extremely influential in establishing the important Californian garlic-growing industry.

Whereas the taboo started in the 18th century as a middle-class attempt to mark themselves out from the lower classes, it was to be the middle classes themselves in the 20th century who started using garlic as a mark of their sophistication and extensive travel. No doubt, as the food writer Jane Grigson noted, standards of hygiene improved in the 20th century, and diets and digestion with them, so the issue of

MYTHS, FOLKLORE AND MEDICINE

Throughout their long history, all manner of special powers have been attributed to the onion family, especially to garlic, and many myths and taboos have built up around them. To some extent these have grown out of the alliums' potent medicinal properties.

ALLIUMS IN MYTH AND FOLKLORE

Priests, shamans and healers have used alliums throughout the ages, and it is inevitable that the onion family has been attributed mystical powers. The ancient Egyptians considered that the layered structure of the onion made it a symbol of eternity, and they were certainly aware of the onion's curative powers. For the Egyptians, the onion not only cured disease and gave vitality, it also replicated the cycle of life itself. As such, it was also a fertility symbol: used in tombs to grant souls a fertile afterlife; used to ascertain female fertility; and denied to priests who might be incited to lustful acts of procreation if they ate onions.

For the Greeks, too, alliums were bestowed with sacred significance and linked to the afterlife. Theophrastus records that garlic should be placed on the side of the road at crossroads as a gift to placate Hecate, goddess of the Underworld, and this practice was continued well into the 11th century AD when the Christian Church put a stop to it. In Homer's *Odyssey*, the power of an onion (probably *Allium moly*) allows Odysseus to enter the lair of Circe. A well-known creation myth of Turkish Muslims records that, when the devil was expelled from Paradise and fell to earth, garlic sprung up where his left foot landed and onions from where his right foot came to rest. An Indian legend concerning the origins of garlic tells that when King Rahu, lord of the demons, stole the elixir of life and was punished by the god Vishnu by being decapitated, garlic sprang from where his blood fell. To this day, the followers of Vishnu refuse to eat any alliums.

From ancient times, onions have always had something of a diabolic, other-worldly connection, but they also suggest the triumph of life over death.

Above: The many different members of the onion family, including garlic, leeks, shallots and chives, all contain allicins – compounds which are believed to have natural antibacterial and antifungal properties.

The devil in onions, present in their fiery bite and effect on the palate, was also thought to incite men to lust and carnal desires. Again and again during the Middle Ages, a connection is made between eating onions, drinking alcohol and sexual incontinence. Or, as Thomas Nashe put it in his book *The Unfortunate Traveller* (1594) "Garlic ... makes a man winke, drinke and stinke". This attitude towards the alliums persisted beyond the Middle Ages in cultures as disparate as Imperial China, caste-structured India and 19th-century Britain.

All these beliefs come into play in one of the best-known myths that surround the allium family – that of the vampire. This myth began in the 16th century in central and eastern Europe but culminates in Bram Stoker's late 19th-century classic, *Dracula*.

Above: In country districts, strings of garlic, such as these sold by a French garlic seller, were often hung on thresholds or on children's cradles to ward off evil spirits.

In the vampire myths, garlic wards off evil and protects potential victims against the undead. Traditionally, in Romania, garlic was used in amulets to protect against the evil eye. In Stoker's *Dracula*, the threshold, windows and hearth are all rubbed and strewn with garlic flowers to prevent Dracula from entering his victim's bed chamber. The hero is also offered garlic as a protective talisman by the peasants on his way to visit Dracula's castle.

In the 19th and 20th centuries, the story becomes a sexual allegory: virgins may protect themselves against male desire by using garlic – men do not like the objects of their desire to smell of garlic. Garlic's part in the Dracula myths brings together all the various qualities ascribed to the "stinking rose" through history. In this story we find garlic's other-worldly, dark associations; garlic's connection with sexuality and desire; garlic's quality as a life force in the face of death; and even its ability to fight off infection as a natural antibiotic.

THE ALLIUMS IN MEDICINE

Alliins, the chemical compounds that create allicins, which give all onions their characteristic smell, are also the source of their remarkable medicinal and curative qualities. Alliins are the thioallyl or sulphur compounds present in all alliums. These compounds are volatile, which means that they break down when any part of the plant is cut or bruised. When the cell walls are damaged and exposed to the air, the compounds are converted by enzyme action to diallydisulphides or allicins – which work as effective antibacterial and antifungal agents. Of the everyday culinary alliums, garlic, with its naturally low water content, has the highest concentration of alliins (1–2 per cent) and hence the greatest medicinal value.

Throughout history the health-giving properties of all the alliums, especially garlic, have been recognized by many writers and many cultures, especially in folk-medicine and herbalism. Garlic was thought of so highly as a medicinal herb that Galen, the Greek medical codifier of the 2nd century AD, labelled it the

Above: The ancient Egyptian Eber Codex, The Book of the Dead, *suggests garlic as a remedy for a wide variety of medical problems.*

poor man's theriac, or cure-all. This passed into medieval English as the "poor man's treacle" (or treat-all), and for many centuries garlic was used to treat a great variety of complaints. As John Trevisa, the 13th-century writer, says, "it [garlic] is cleped tryacle of cherles among auctours in olde tyme".

Early medicinal uses

The earliest texts to mention the use of onions as medicine are the 5,000-year-old Ayurvedic texts from India. Garlic is mentioned as a useful treatment for digestive disorders, throat and bronchial complaints and even for typhoid. The Egyptian *Eber Codex, The Book of the Dead*, is a medical work of therapies and cures from around 1550 BC. Garlic is again mentioned here as useful for treating many complaints as diverse as headaches and the pains of childbirth. Throughout the classical and medieval period, writers again and again extol the curative properties of the alliums. The most common complaints mentioned include chest and bronchial problems

(Nero was not alone in thinking alliums improved the voice), worms, intestinal problems, bladder problems and lack of libido. They were also used to treat open wounds, to guard against infection from animal bites and to treat colds, headaches, haemorrhoids, sunburn and even leprosy.

The Greek Hippocrates (*c*.400 BC), the father of modern medicine, thought garlic good for wounds and toothache. Dioscorides, the Greek doctor who travelled with the Roman army (which was largely fed on onions, leeks and garlic) in the 1st century AD, notes its use against tapeworms and snake bites. He was also convinced that garlic could help clear the arteries and cure coughs. Pliny the Elder (AD 23–79) in his *Historia Naturalis* gives over 60 garlic remedies, including cures for bites by wild animals and low libido. This latter is a common theme in the use of garlic, and links in with the idea that all the onions excite the carnal appetites.

Right: An early illustration of garlic (Allium sativum) *showing the flowers and the mature bulb.*

Below: Hippocrates, the father of modern medicine, praised the healing powers of garlic and posited it as a cure for a great number of diverse ailments.

Allium sativum L.

Medieval medicine and beyond

These notions held by the Greeks survived well into the Middle Ages. The 14th-century French herbal *The Four Seasons of the House of Cerruti* claims that white onions help to bring forth milk in nursing mothers and promote virile semen in men, and the herbal also considers garlic to be an undoubted aphrodisiac. Food historian John Ayto quotes an observation from *Andrew Boorde's Dietary of Helthe* (1542), which claims that "onions do promote a man to veneryous [sexual] actes", much as the Roman writer Pliny had done centuries earlier.

Medical thought and practice was governed throughout the Middle Ages by the doctrine of the humours, which explained how humans interacted with the natural world. The humours were the four bodily fluids: blood, choler, melancholy and phlegm, which were thought to determine character and physical health. The four elements of fire, water, air and earth also had characteristic qualities: hot, moist, cold and dry respectively. All living things – plants, animals, human beings – were governed by one or more elements and displayed one, or a combination of, these qualities.

Onions were considered hot and moist and were thought to govern the blood, the humour of the sanguine personality. Garlic was considered hotter and drier and thought to be good for treating the cold and wet phlegmatic personality. In John Trevisa's 13th-century translation of *De Proprietatibus Rerum,* he says of garlic "if colerik men ete to moche therof it maketh the body to hoot ... and is cause of madnesse and of frenesye", but later he admits its use: "and garlek abateth the ache of guttes aboute the reynes [period pains] also". John Evelyn, in his *Acetaria* (1699), observed that garlic was "dry toward excess ... and more proper for our northern rustics, especially [those] living in uliginous and moist places. Whereas leeks are hot, and of vertue

prolifick ... the Welch, who eat them much, are observ'd to be very fruitful". In the doctrine of humours, a plant's fecundity is thought to reflect its good effect on human fertility.

Other cultures also developed systems of categorizing the natural world and hence food. In China, the alliums are yang in the yin-yang balance of properties. Yang foods are male, dry and hot so, during the T'ang Dynasty (AD 618–907), garlic was endorsed as good for heating the blood and as a tonic. The Iranian "Araqi" classification ranks garlic as one of the hottest foods.

The alliums, especially garlic, have repeatedly been mentioned for use as treatments for open wounds, bites by venomous snakes and wild animals and cleansing the blood. Trevisa writes in

Above: Nicholas Culpeper, the 17th-century apothecary, extolled the curative virtues of onions and other alliums in his popular herbal, The English Physician.

the 13th century that garlic has "many maner vertu yfounde ... to putte out venym and all venemous thinges". Thomas Tusser, the 16th-century writer of agricultural doggerel, says that "now leeks are in season, for pottage full good and spareth the milch-cow, and purgeth the blood". Nicholas Culpepper in his well-known 17th-century herbal remarks that onions "Provoke urine and women's courses, helps the biting of mad dogs and other venonmous creatures ... [it] kills the worms".

There is also evidence that, in pre-Colonial America, native Americans used roasted wild onions and honey to neutralize snakebites and to help heal open wounds. Even as late as World War I (1914–18) garlic was used by the British as an antiseptic on a large scale, as noted by Mrs Grieve in her *Modern Herbal* (1931). The garlic was pounded to express the juice, which was then applied on swabs to open wounds to help staunch bleeding and prevent the wound from becoming infected.

Left: This medieval illustration shows the harvesting and bunching of garlic, which was believed to be good for treating a phlegmatic personality.

Alliums as preventives

In general, onions and garlic have been considered to be preventives and act as a general tonic against both infection and infestation. They are mentioned as preventives in outbreaks of the plague, for instance, both in France and England. The alliums' prophylactic properties were often linked with their use as talismans to ward off disease, rather than as remedies to be imbibed or rubbed on the body.

The Egyptian *Eber Codex* advocates wearing garlic around the neck as a way of driving out tapeworms. Greek and Macedonian mothers hung garlic around their babies' necks or cradles to ward off disease. In ancient China, onions, garlic and bunching onions were considered part of the "five strong-smelling foods" (*wu han*) and were hung on red cords at the threshold to protect the household against disease. John Evelyn (1699) considered garlic "a

charm against all infection and poyson", even though he despised it in salads. Pre-colonial native Americans considered that wild onions worn around the neck protected the wearer from colds and bronchitis. Most famously, of course, a garland of garlic was supposed to guard the wearer against being attacked by a vampire. Even in garlic-phobic Japan, in the northern town of Tsukuba-Khinoya, there is an annual festival, which dates from the Heian period of more than 1,000 years ago, when garlic is hung at the entrance to the house to prevent disease crossing the threshold during the coming year.

Alliums in the modern diet

Many contemporary writers consider that the onion family, particularly garlic, should be an essential part of our diet. Alliums aid good digestion, maintain a balanced blood pressure and work as a general tonic to help stave off infection. Recent research seems to confirm most of the herbalist lore that has built up through the ages.

Left: With the growing interest in the healing potential of food, organically grown food, such as these leeks, is becoming more popular.

Below: Of all the members of the onion family, garlic, in particular, is renowned for its healing properties.

Above: Links have been made between garlic and cancer prevention, and experts agree that even a small amount every day will help strengthen the immune system.

There is evidence that garlic reduces blood pressure, helps lower LDL (low-density lipo-protein) cholesterol and may prevent the build-up of cholesterol within the arteries. Raw garlic has always been considered an effective antibiotic. There is evidence that although garlic is not so strong as modern antibiotics, the way in which it works is so different that it can kill strains of bacteria that have become antibiotic-resistant. Garlic and onions generally have great antifungal and antiviral properties, and they play their part in maintaining a healthy intestinal flora and fauna.

Research is also progressing to examine the link between garlic and cancer. Garlic certainly has antioxidant properties and contains selenium, which is known to strengthen the body's ability to resist cancer. Clinical tests have also shown that garlic reduces the size of certain tumours in animals or prevents them from growing. Most experts agree that even a small amount of garlic every day – say one clove – will help maintain good health and strengthen the immune system. Garlic can also help thin the blood and prevent blood clotting.

Lore, remedies and old wives' tales

• As a remedy for corns, bandage a cut slice of garlic over the corn and replace it every day until the corn drops off.

• A syrup made from garlic steeped in vinegar and honey is good for asthma, coughs and general bronchial problems.

• To soothe a dry and painful cough, take a spoonful of honey mixed with a little crushed raw onion or garlic.

• It was once recommended that a roasted onion be applied to the affected ear as a cure for earache; it was also said to be good for boils.

• All onions are good for getting rid of moles in the garden. Drop peeled garlic or cut onions into their holes.

• Chopped garlic, bandaged to the soles of the feet and renewed daily, was thought a remedy for smallpox and even leprosy.

• Cut garlic rubbed over the lips will prevent them being burned by the sun.

• Mixed with lard or white cooking fat and applied to the chest or back as a poultice, garlic is thought good for chest conditions.

• A cut onion will rid a room of other strong smells, such as paint.

• An Irish folk-belief is that garlic planted on a Good Friday will protect people from fever during the whole year.

• A cut onion is said to attract all infection from the air into it and will kill air-borne infection.

• To cure baldness, rub the sap of a cut onion mixed with honey on the bald patch until the skin reddens – then wait.

• According to Brewer's *Dictionary of Phrase & Fable*, the phrase "to know your onions" is probably derived from Cockney rhyming slang, as in "onion rings" – "things". However, some have suggested that it refers to the man who edited the *Oxford English Dictionary* – C. T. Onions.

THE WORLD OF ONIONS

While we tend to think of onions as being more or less the same, there are many different

varieties, colours and sizes. Some are better suited to roasting, others to frying; some are

delicious cooked whole, others are better for chopping, slicing and eating raw. The same is

true of the other members of the onion family — especially shallots, garlic and leeks.

This fully illustrated reference section will help you to identify all the main varieties

of edible alliums and give guidance on how best to use them in the kitchen.

THE ALLIUM FAMILY

There are more than 300 distinct species in the allium family, many of which have been used as food plants. For culinary purposes the best-known species are the onion (*Allium cepa*), the shallot (*Allium cepa*, Aggregatum Group), the leek (*Allium ampeloprasum* var. *porrum*), bunching onions (*Allium fistulosum* and *Allium cepa*, Proliferum Group), garlic (*Allium sativum*) and, finally, the various chives (*Allium schoenoprasum* and *Allium tuberosum*).

Onions, shallots, leeks and garlic are commonly known only in their cultivated forms. Although we do not know the wild forms of many of these plants, we can make informed guesses as to their origins. Many wild forms of edible alliums still exist around the world, as well as many varieties of allium that are purely ornamental.

The one thing that connects all the members of the allium family is their characteristic smell. Alliums contain chemical compounds known as alliins. When a plant is bruised or damaged, the alliins immediately begin to break down into the sulphur compounds known as allicins, which produce the instantly recognizable smell and flavour. The release of these volatile compounds can make us cry when we chop onions. If you wander through a woodland carpeted with wild garlic (*Allium ursinum*) in the late spring, the acrid,

pungent smell is almost overpowering. Place a bunch of unwrapped garlic chives in the refrigerator, and you will find that within a few hours the eggs, milk and butter will be tainted with their strong smell. Onions are some of the most potent flavouring ingredients available for use in the kitchen, so it is no wonder they have been used by cooks for countless generations.

WILD ALLIUMS

Ramsons (*Allium ursinum*) are one of the commonest wild alliums in Britain and they grow in damp, shady areas throughout Europe. They form broad, fresh green leaves and have lacy heads of white flowers in late spring. The whole plant is very odorous and will affect the milk of any goats or cattle that graze on it. Ramsons used to be fed to chickens before they started laying, as a spring tonic and to "kick-start" them into productivity. The leaves are good wrapped around fish before cooking over charcoal. The flowers may be added to salads, and young leaves may be shredded into omelettes or rice dishes; they were commonly used in place of scarce onions during World War II. Ramsons have left their mark in a number of English place names, such as Ramsbottom in Lancashire and Ramsey on the Isle of Man.

Rocambole *Allium scorodoprasum* and *Allium sativum* var. *ophioscorodon* have both been called rocambole. The first is commonly called the sand leek, for it likes to grow in sandy soils; the second is a form of garlic. Both have coiled or twisted stems and grow widely across Europe. They have a good, mild flavour and were once exceedingly popular in salads and for flavouring cheese. John Evelyn, the 17th-century diarist and gardener who was quite against garlic, thought rocambole far more socially acceptable: "a clove or two of roccombo, of a yet milder and delicate nature, which by rubbing the [salad] dish only, imparts its vertue agreeably enough" (*Acetaria*, 1699).

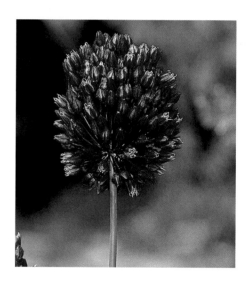

Above: The pink-flowered wild sand leek has a mild, garlic flavour, which has been popular with cooks for centuries.

Babbington leek or kurrat (*Allium ampeloprasum* var. *babbingtonii* or *Allium ampeloprasum* var. *kurrat*) is probably related to the elephant garlic (*Allium ampeloprasum*). It is grown in the Near East for its narrow leaves. The sectioned bulb may be used as a mild version of garlic.

Other wild onions that have been used in the kitchen are crow garlic (*Allium vineale*) in Europe; *A. canadense*, *A. tricconum* and *A. cernum* in America.

Left: The flowers of ramsons can be found in European woodlands in spring.

ONIONS

These are all varieties of *Allium cepa*. Onions are grown for the bulb, formed by layers of fleshy, swollen leaf bases; the actual stem of an onion is the small layer of hard tissue at the top of the roots. The onion probably originated in western and central Asia, in an area stretching from modern-day Israel to India, and has been cultivated since the earliest times. It is likely that various kinds of onion were first cultivated around the Middle and Near East.

The uses of onions in the kitchen are myriad. They are used in the savoury cooking of almost every country and culture. They are fried, boiled, roasted, baked, stuffed and grilled (broiled).

There are many different kinds of onion and they are classified for kitchen use according to size, shape and colour.

Yellow onions

These are the most usual type of onion and are characterized by a light brown skin and a greenish white to pale yellow flesh. There are different varieties within this basic type, but they are commonly known as Spanish onions, regardless of their place of origin; Bermuda is the similar generic title for this kind of large, mild onion in the United States. For culinary purposes, Spanish onions are usually large, round and mild. Other types of yellow onions include brown onions, which have thick brown skins, and French onions, which have a

Left: Spanish (Bermuda) onions are usually large and have a mild flavour.

stronger flavour. Generally, the younger and greener the onion, the more pungent the flesh. Several varieties of yellow onion have been favoured for the mild sweetness of their flesh, such as the Vidalia from the north-western states of America and the Maui from Hawaii. The Walla Walla, named after the town in Washington State where it was first grown, was brought to the United States by Corsican immigrants in the early 20th century. Most onions in the northern hemisphere are autumn- cropping from a spring sowing, but some varieties have been bred to overwinter from an autumn sowing and crop in summer. Of these, the Japanese varieties are best known in Europe. The Vidalia is a summer-cropping onion in America.

Below: Brown onions have a thick, brown skin.

Above: French onions tend to have a stronger, more pungent flavour than Spanish (Bermuda) onions.

Uses in the kitchen Yellow onions are suitable for most kitchen purposes. Choose large round onions for baking, stuffing or cutting into rings. Longer or squatter onions are better for slicing or roasting whole. Some people consider them too strong to eat raw, although a mild yellow onion is good in potato salad or in marinated fish dishes, such as ceviche and soused herrings.

Uses in the kitchen

Red onions usually have a much milder, sweeter flavour than yellow onions and they are popular in salads; this is, no doubt, also because of their attractive pink-tinged flesh. They are frequently used raw in salsas, relishes, antipasti and marinated dishes. Red onions are also good roasted, either whole or cut into wedges, which concentrates the sweetness of their flesh. They are less useful for basic frying, when they have less flavour than other varieties and their lovely pink colour tends to turn to a murky mauve or dull brown.

Above: Red onions have beautiful purple-red skins and pink-tinged, mild flavoured flesh that is excellent in salads and salsas.

Red onions

As with yellow onions, there is a great variety of size and shape among red onions, but all are characterized by shiny, papery skins of a glorious purple-red. The flesh is basically white, stained red at the edges of each layer. The colour is released by contact with acids, such as vinegar or citrus juice, and red onion slices tossed in vinegar will soon turn a beautiful, uniform deep pink.

White onions

These are usually medium to large onions with a papery, white outer skin and white flesh. They tend not to vary so much in size, shape and flavour as yellow and red onions. They are usually fairly strong in taste.

Uses in the kitchen White onions may be used for all general cooking purposes, although many people consider them too strong for eating raw. Their even size and shape make them good for baking whole or stuffing.

Cipolla or borettane onions

These are quite small, flattish or squat onions with a pale golden skin and pale yellow flesh, while some varieties are tinged with pink. Cipolla or borettane onions are popular in Italy and some varieties are grown in France, too. They have an excellent, sweet flavour combined with an agreeable strength of taste.

Left: Evenly shaped white onions have a stronger flavour than red onions and are good for stuffing.

Right: A string of mixed onions makes an attractive sight hanging in a cool spot, and will cover all your onion needs in the kitchen.

Left: Cipolla onions are common in Italian markets and are excellent for braising, pickling and in salads.

Above: Small yellow pickling onions are good for adding whole to stews and casseroles.

Uses in the kitchen

Because they are generally small and have such a characteristic shape it would be a shame to use these onions for slicing or chopping so, generally, they are peeled and cooked whole. They are excellent caramelized or cooked *à la grecque* in a mixture of olive oil, wine and spices. They are also excellent for roasting whole, bottling and pickling.

Below: Tiny silverskin onions have a strong flavour and crisp texture.

Pickling onions

This is a general term for many different varieties of small onion. Some varieties may simply be immature yellow or red onions; others have been specially bred to produce small onions.

White silverskin pickling onions These strong-flavoured tiny "pearl" onions are nearly always used for pickling. When a small, pickled silverskin onion is added to a Martini, the drink is called a Gibson.

Yellow and red pickling onions These are usually larger and milder than the silverskin varieties. They also keep much better than silverskins. Store them as you would normal onions.

Uses in the kitchen These onions are excellent for pickling whole in spiced vinegar and for roasting whole, or for caramelizing. Small onions are good added whole to casseroles and stews. Typically, the bourguignonne garnish, characteristic of the cooking of Burgundy in France, uses fried onions and small mushrooms to finish stews.

Grelots

This is the French term for small, flattish onions with a green skin and very white flesh. They are very like a bulbous spring onion (scallion). Various types of this kind of fresh onion (they must be eaten fresh as they will not store well) are often labelled salad onions in supermarkets and food stores. They have a generally mild-flavoured flesh with a crisp bite.

Uses in the kitchen Grelots are used extensively sliced raw in salads, but are good in many quick-cooked dishes, such as omelettes and frittatas, or sliced into stir-fries. They are less useful for general frying or long-cooked recipes, when they tend to disintegrate.

Below: Pickling onions are favourites for traditional English pickled onions.

SHALLOTS

These are a distinct sub-species of *Allium cepa*, and are grouped botanically under the umbrella term Aggregatum Group, from the Latin meaning "a whole formed from several units". This is what distinguishes shallots from onions: they form clusters of several bulbs at the leaf bases. Their name comes from the ancient Palestinian port of Ascalon (now the port of Ashkelon in southern Israel), where it is thought they were first grown, but it is more likely to have been the port from where they were first exported to Rome. There is quite a variety of different shallots, but most are smaller than onions, composed of finer layers and they contain less water. As a result, they have a more concentrated flavour than onions, which makes them useful in the kitchen.

Banana shallots are the largest variety and get their name from their elongated shape. They have a smooth tan skin and a slightly milder flavour than other shallots.

Pink shallots and *échalote grise* are perhaps the most strongly flavoured shallots and are the most popular varieties in France. Pink shallots have a reddish

Left: Banana shallots (or frog's leg shallots) are large and mild, and may be used in the same way as small onions in most recipes.

skin and pink-tinged flesh; *échalote grise* are paler, but still have a pinkish cast to the flesh. They have a crisp texture and pungent, but not harsh, flavour, which is good raw and cooked.

Brown, English or Dutch shallots are probably the most common shallots found in food stores. These small, tan-skinned shallots often separate into subsidiary bulbs when they are peeled. They are good general-purpose shallots with well-flavoured but reasonably mild flesh.

Asian or Thai red shallots are small, round red bulbs, which are used extensively in the cooking of many South-east Asian countries. They vary from the strong to exceptionally strong in taste and are used most commonly in spice pastes, when they are pounded with other ingredients. Because of their low water content they are also excellent for slicing and frying to make crisp-fried shallots, which are common as a garnish on Thai salads and curries.

Chinese "shallots" are actually a different species (*Allium chinense*) and not a shallot at all. It is a wild species that is cultivated in China (*jiao tou* in Cantonese or *rakkyo* in Japanese).

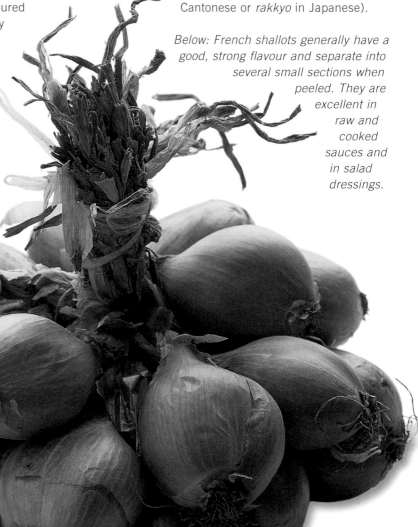

Below: French shallots generally have a good, strong flavour and separate into several small sections when peeled. They are excellent in raw and cooked sauces and in salad dressings.

Left: Pink Thai shallots are used extensively in Thai curry pastes and are also used as salad garnishes. They are exceptionally pretty pickled in rice vinegar with herbs and spices.

Uses in the kitchen Shallots are excellent roasted whole, caramelized or pickled. Raw, they are essential in salad dressings and a wide range of French dishes. Chopped raw shallot is often sprinkled over a seared, rare steak *à la bordelaise*. Cooked, shallots are an essential ingredient in many sauces that need the flavour of onion but not its bulk. Shallots have a low water content, which means that they can burn and toughen easily, so care should be taken when frying. Potato onions may be used like ordinary onions.

They are grown mainly for pickling, and that is the form in which they are usually seen in the West.

Potato onions are related to shallots and belong to the Aggregatum Group of *Allium cepa*. The species is peculiar among the onions in that it develops entirely underground, in the same way as garlic. Because of this, it is a little hardier than other onions and shallots and, in the past, it was often planted in autumn. It forms clumps of small, yellow-skinned onions that store well. As many as eight small onions may form per clump.

Potato onions were once far more popular than they are now, especially in the mild west of England and Ireland, from where they were taken to the United States. They filled a gap between the end of the stored autumn-cropping onions and the new crop of shallots in late summer. Today, the potato onion is regarded as a bit of an oddity, mainly restricted to the herb patch, but the bulbs are of good flavour and are just as useful as ordinary onions in the kitchen. It is an interesting rarity that keen gardener-cooks might like to consider growing.

Right: English or Dutch shallots are generally brown skinned and have a mild flavour.

LEEKS

As a cultivated vegetable, the leek has even more ancient origins than the onion. It is probably derived from the wild *Allium ampeloprasum*, although some botanists call it a species in its own right (*Allium porrum*). The wild leek is a native of the Mediterranean and islands such as the Azores, Madeira and the Canaries. This wild leek has been traced back as far as Jericho 7,000 years ago. "Leeks" of a different species – *Allium ramosum* – have also been cultivated in China for thousands of years. Although there are many hundreds of varieties of cultivated leek, in fact, they vary only in size and winter hardiness. Some leeks have been bred to grow to vast dimensions and others to withstand quite severe winter frosts.

In the kitchen, the cook is mainly concerned with size. Traditionally in the northern hemisphere, leeks have been seen as a winter vegetable. These large leeks are one of the few vegetables to survive outdoors without protection. In recent years, baby leeks have increased in popularity, and while these may simply be immature, miniature versions of ordinary leeks, there are now special

Below: Baby leeks are good for serving whole. Steam, then brown in a hot griddle pan to bring out their flavour.

varieties that are grown to mature quickly and provide slender, tender leeks throughout the summer.

In leeks, the "bulb" or layers of leaf base are elongated to form what is commonly regarded as a stem, although botanically the stem is strictly the sometimes slightly bulbous base of the leek just above the roots. The leek divides into the white, fleshy basal portion and the green leaves or "flags". All the fleshy part of the leek may be used, but the green part is tougher and requires more cooking. Leeks have an almost universally popular flavour that is both milder and more rounded than that of onions. It lacks the pungency of onions, but makes up for it in the gentle depth of its flavour.

Uses in the kitchen Young, fresh leeks may be used raw, shredded in salads (a favourite with the Romans), but their chief use in the kitchen is when they are cooked. They are superlative in soups. Leeks cook more quickly than onions, so they should be added to stews towards the end of cooking. Whole, they are good braised or blanched then grilled (broiled). Baby leeks are usually cooked whole. They are excellent briefly boiled or steamed, then dressed in oil and vinegar.

Below: Large leeks, with their sweet, mild flavour, are among the most popular of alliums in the modern kitchen. They are excellent in soups and cooked salads.

SPRING ONIONS

Most of what are sold as spring or salad onions (scallions in the United States) are simply early-maturing varieties of onion (*Allium cepa*). However, the need for a year-round supply and recent breeding, especially by the Japanese, means that some spring onion varieties now have genes from Welsh onions (*Allium fistulosum*) in their makeup. If the cross-section of the leaf is circular, then the onion is a variety based on *Allium fistulosum*; if the cross-section of the leaf is crescent-shaped, then it is derived from *Allium cepa*.

As the English name suggests, these onions probably started out as the spring thinnings from ordinary onions. In culinary terms, the distinction between the different types of spring onion is purely one of size – they vary from the really tiny (thinner than a pencil) to those that are as large as, if not larger than, a baby leek. Some varieties of spring onion have a markedly bulbous base, and show a relation to the type of salad onions the French call *grelotes*; others are more leek-like, with no particular basal swelling.

Spring onions have a mild, sweet flavour with a fresh green snap, which makes them good in salads. Use thinner spring onions for salads and thicker ones for cooking. Red spring onions have been developed: these look pretty in salads, but do not differ significantly in flavour from white spring onions.

Left: Bulb spring onions (scallions) are the best ones to use for grilling (broiling) whole or for cooking in stir-fries, or deep-frying whole in batter.

Uses in the kitchen In Britain, spring onions have traditionally been served whole (trimmed) in salads. They are good as crudités with a black olive tapenade and are excellent chopped or sliced into mixed or composite salads; they are widely used like this in the Middle East. They are a good addition to Mexican salsas. Spring onions are also excellent cooked, and are an essential ingredient in Asian stir-fries because they cook quickly. They grill (broil) well, taking only a few minutes to cook. In Cataluña, in north-east Spain, they are widely used in this way: known as *calçots*, they are grilled over hot coals and served with all sorts of grilled meats and a nut/chilli sauce called *salsa romesco*. The tops of young spring onions may be used as a garnish in the same way as chives, and spring onions curls and brushes are popular garnishes in Chinese food.

Below: Thin spring onions (scallions) are excellent in salads, whether left whole or chopped small.

BUNCHING, WELSH AND TREE ONIONS

Bunching or Welsh onions (*Allium fistulosum*) are very popular in China and Japan. They are called Welsh as a corruption of the Germanic *welsche*, meaning foreign. This label was probably given when they were first introduced into Europe from Asia. In Wales itself they used to be known as "holtzers" and they were once a popular flavouring because they grew in early spring when few other vegetables were available. They are also known as *chiboules* or *cibols*. In Chinese cooking, they are used in stir-fries in place of spring onions (scallions). The onion grows in clusters of bulbs, so individual onions may be removed, leaving the plant growing. The flavour is mild.

Right: Tree onions, or Egyptian onions, are vigorous, clumping onions that grow well in the herb patch.

Below: Bunching or Welsh onions are the most popular type of onion in China and Japan.

Tree onions (*Allium cepa*, Proliferum Group) are true perennials for the herb patch. As with bunching onions, individual onions may be removed from the plant for use in the kitchen. Tree onions also form little bulblets at the tips of the stem, which may also be used in the kitchen or may be planted to form new plants. A particularly vigorous and tall form of the tree onion, known as the Catawissa onion, was a popular pot herb in America during the 19th and early 20th centuries.

Uses in the kitchen Both the basal stem and the green flags may be used in sauces, stir-fries and salads, but because tree onions are slightly tougher than spring onions, they do not grill (broil) well. The bulblets are good chopped in sauces and salad dressings.

Above: Chive flowers have a surprisingly oniony flavour and make a pretty addition to salads in early summer.

CHIVES

European chive (*Allium schoenoprasum*) is a common wild plant, occurring from northern Russia to the Mediterranean and as far east as the Himalayas. Various larger-growing varieties have been selected for domestication. Chives are one of the first herbs to start into growth in the early spring, and the first shoots are remarkably strong and pungent; later on, as the plants develop, they become milder. The flowers also have a mild oniony taste and are good in salads and as a garnish. Chives are usually eaten raw or very lightly cooked.

Chinese chives (*Allium tuberosum*) are also known as *kuchai* (*gow choy* in Cantonese) or garlic chives. They have a much more pungent smell and taste than European chives and because of their strong flavour are usually cooked. They come in two forms: the leaf form has flat, slightly twisted leaves with a pronounced garlic smell; the flowering stalk with a round, hollow stem is normally sold with flower buds intact. A third kind, Chinese yellow chives (*gow wong*), are simply a version of Chinese chives that have been blanched by excluding all natural light. They are highly regarded by the Chinese as a vegetable in their own right for stir-

frying. Garlic shoots are also used in Chinese cookery and are sometimes known as garlic chives.

Uses in the kitchen European chives are widely used as a garnish, but they have a surprising amount of flavour, especially when picked young from the garden. They are excellent in egg and cheese dishes, but care should be taken that they are not left in contact with eggs or dairy products as they will taint them. Chives are useful for adding a mild oniony taste to salad dressings, soups and sauces, and are particularly good in potato dishes. Chinese chives are more robust and need brief cooking. They are excellent in stir-fries, in rice dishes and stirred into soups and stews.

Right: Chinese chives are often sold in tight bud and may be chopped and used in stir-fries.

*Below: Chives (*Allium schoenoprasum*) are popular throughout Europe and North America, and give a mild, oniony flavour that is particularly good in cheese and egg dishes.*

GARLIC

At various times, garlic (*Allium sativum*) has been the most lauded and the most despised of all the onion tribe because it is the fieriest and most pungent. It is one of the few culinary alliums that forms its bulb underground rather than on the surface of the soil.

Typically, a garlic bulb, or head, is formed of several separate cloves, each wrapped in its own papery skin, and the whole head is enclosed in a further papery skin. Garlic is widely cultivated, but needs a long growing season and a period of cold weather to initiate proper bulb development.

Most cultures consider it a herb or flavouring rather than a vegetable in its own right, but many dishes exist that include several whole heads of garlic rather than the odd clove that more timid cooks employ. A whole head of garlic, gently roasted until it becomes sweet, mellow and purée-soft, may easily be consumed by one person at a sitting. There are French recipes for chicken or lamb with forty cloves of garlic, which achieved an almost mythical status in garlic-phobic Britain of the 1950s. Some Asian dishes contain huge quantities of garlic by Western standards, such as southern Indian dishes of whole garlic cloves cooked with spices and coconut milk.

Left: Young, new-season or wet garlic that has not been dried has a particularly sweet and mild flavour.

There are many different varieties of garlic, most of them geographically specific and therefore adapted to local climate and conditions. Garlic stores well when it is dried, but has a different taste from when it is used green and freshly pulled. There are some garlics with very white skin, while others are stained or mottled deep pink. Some garlic varieties separate naturally into tiny cloves, while others are characterized by large, fat cloves. Generally, the larger and less dried the clove, the milder and less pungent it is, but this is not an unbroken rule.

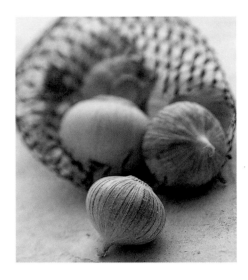

Above: Solo garlic is a mild form of garlic in which each small bulb comprises a single clove.

Below: Garlic is often sold in strings and will keep for several months if hung in a cool, dry place.

Middle East and in all Mediterranean countries. Crisp, fried garlic is a popular garnish to Burmese food, and in both Thailand and Korea pickled garlic is an accompaniment to many meals.

Garlic alters in flavour according to how it is prepared and for how long it is cooked. Crushed garlic, either raw or briefly cooked, is the most pungent and strongly flavoured; a whole head of garlic, slowly roasted, will have a mellow, nutty, toasty flavour. Garlic may be fried, baked, roasted or braised. It is a ubiquitous ingredient in most spice pastes, Spanish salsas, Italian pestos and Mexican moles. It is also widely used in all types of cuisine in dressings, marinades, soups and stews.

Left: Smoked garlic is infused (steeped) over wood smoke. It is good in garlic mayonnaise, marinades and dressings.

Below: There are many different kinds of garlic, which are often geographically specific: white garlic is popular in California. California Late and Silverskin are well-known varieties.

Elephant garlic (*Allium ampeloprasm*) There is some confusion in food stores between this variety and large-growing varieties of true garlic. Elephant garlic is actually more closely related to the leek than to garlic proper. It has a mild, creamy, garlic flavour and the cloves are very large in comparison with ordinary garlic. Another variety of allium (*Allium gigantum*) has also been known as elephant garlic, but most gardeners grow this as an ornamental, for its very large, purple drumstick flowers, rather than as a food plant.

Solo is a variety of garlic that has been specially bred to develop just one, large clove, making it easy to peel and prepare. It is useful for dishes using a lot of garlic, but expensive to use in any quantity. The flavour is fairly mild.

Wet or new season garlic may simply be labelled "fresh" or "green" garlic. Typically, in the northern hemisphere, this is ready in late spring to early summer, when the papery skin has not fully developed and dried out. Usually the head is used whole: it is creamy white, streaked and flushed with green and pink, and has a delicious mild flavour that is ideal for European garlic soups and to roast whole.

Smoked garlic usually consists of large, whole heads of garlic that have been hot-smoked so that they are partly cooked and infused (steeped) with wood smoke. They have a light, tan-brown exterior skin that should be peeled before the cloves are used for crushing into mayonnaise, for making garlic butter, or for tossing with pasta.

Garlic shoots – the first shoots of early spring – are considered a great delicacy in many areas of southern Europe (Italy, France and Spain) and are used in much the same way as chives or spring onions (scallions). They are also much used in Chinese stir-fries. Soup made from garlic shoots is a great favourite and is considered a splendid health tonic – a sort of "spring clean" for the blood and circulation. The shoots are also pickled for use later in the season in relishes, salads and sauces.

Uses in the kitchen Garlic is an almost universal favourite for flavouring in cuisines all around the world. It is widely used, both raw and cooked, to flavour all kinds of dishes. It is used raw in dressings, salsas, butters and salads. Cooked, it is used in huge quantities in most Asian countries (apart from Japan), Mexico and South America, the

ALLIUM FLAVOURINGS AND INGREDIENTS

There are a large number of allium flavourings and ingredients available. Some are made from onions, while others are not even related to the alliums but impart an oniony flavour.

Asafoetida

This is a pungent spice obtained from a resin from the root of a giant fennel (*Ferula asafoetida*). It is not related to the alliums, but does give a distinct garlicky taste to the dishes in which it is used. It was favoured in Roman cooking and was used by the Roman epicurean Apicius in the 1st century AD. Today, asafoetida is used in Afghanistan, India and Pakistan. It is usually bought ground and should be kept well sealed, because the smell of the uncooked spice is disagreeable. It is used in Indian Brahman cooking in place of the forbidden onions and garlic.

Onion seed or kalonji

The name onion seed is a complete misnomer, because the Indian spice kalonji is not a relation of the alliums, but is related to the familiar, blue-flowered annual "love-in-the-mist" (*Nigella sativa*) of our flower borders. It is much used in India, especially in Bengali cooking. It is good stir-fried with green vegetables, and sprinkled on the top of Indian breads and pancakes.

Dried onion flakes

These are simply dehydrated thin slices of onion, but as onions are available all year round, they are rarely used today. They should be rehydrated in warm water for 15–20 minutes before using, or they may be gently fried, to form crisp fried onions, which are much used as a garnish for Thai salads and curries. Dried shallot flakes are also available.

Crisp fried onion flakes

These are ready-fried crisp scraps of onion, which are useful as a garnish in salads, soups and rice dishes, or may be added to egg dishes. Once the pack is opened, the flakes should be used quickly or they will go rancid.

Left: Pungent asafoetida is much used in Indian vegetarian cooking.

Above right: Dry-roasting kalonji seeds will bring out their nutty flavour.

Right: Fried onion flakes are good sprinkled over salads and rice dishes.

Below: Dried shallot flakes may be added directly to slow-cooked stews.

Garlic salt

This is a mix of dried garlic and salt. It can be used to add instant garlic flavour to dishes such as garlic bread, but the drying process alters garlic's flavour, and many cooks prefer to use fresh garlic.

Garlic pastes

Ready-prepared garlic pastes are widely available. However, as with dried garlic, some of the preservatives used in the preparation of commercial garlic pastes alter the flavour and can give a slightly metallic tang to the finished dish. It is better to make your own roasted garlic paste, which will keep for 1–2 weeks covered with olive oil in a screw-top jar in the refrigerator.

Above left: Garlic salt is used in Cajun cooking for their blackened dishes.

Above: Fried garlic and garlic granules

Below: Small onions, garlic and shallots are popular in pickles.

Right: Minced (ground) garlic

Bottled or pickled alliums

In many countries, onions, garlic and shallots are pickled or bottled in vinegar or oil. These preserved alliums make a delicious addition to mixed salads, egg and rice dishes. Bottled green shoots of sprouting garlic are a popular spring flavouring in Spain, Italy and China. They are occasionally available fresh from Asian food stores.

CULTIVATION

The fact that the onion family has been cultivated since the earliest times and that it has spread far and wide across the globe suggests that onions are easy to grow. This is largely true: for the most part, onions are easily grown, hardy plants that are adaptable to a wide range of climates and soils. Certain varieties have been bred that are more suited to specific climatic conditions, and these different types vary in flavour and strength. Generally, the quicker an onion grows, the milder its flavour will be. Ideal quick-growing conditions, such as those found in large parts of Spain, the west-coast of the United States and Hawaii, foster sweet, mild onions, such as the Vidalia from Washington State and the Maui from the Hawaiian island of the same name. Onions that grow more slowly, say in northern Europe, tend to be stronger and more pungent. Home-grown onions, which have had to survive the

Below: Seedlings of the onion Vera Prima, ready for planting out.

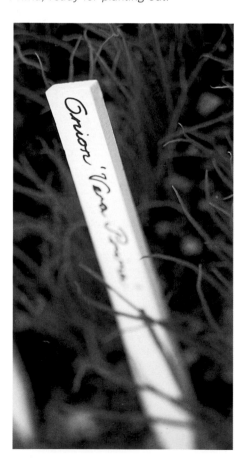

vicissitudes of the garden, possibly with periods of drought and neglect, tend to be stronger in flavour and odour than commercially grown onions, which have led a pampered and well-watered life.

Onions can be grown in almost any type of soil, but most members of the onion family like a friable, open, slightly sandy soil. The best way is to plant in ground that has been manured in the autumn before planting. All members of the onion family prefer an open, sunny position: they do not grow well under the shade of trees or buildings, nor do they like the competition of roots from trees or large shrubs. Onions like to be well fed, but not with a fertilizer with a high nitrogen content, as this will make them grow large leaves rather than foster the formation of the bulb or stem. They also need to be well watered, as this helps the bulb to swell, but they can stand short periods of drought.

Onions (*Allium cepa* vars.) are biennial plants, which means that they form a bulb or storage organ one year, in order to flower and set seed the next. If the climate is mild enough, onions left in the ground during winter will shoot, flower and set seed in late spring.

The gardener grows the onion for the bulb it produces in its first year of growth. If it is properly dried off and stored, this bulb will survive throughout the winter dormant period and will not attempt to grow again until the following spring. Onions that are kept in a place that is too warm or damp may well shoot while they are in storage. An onion that does this is still edible, but the winter dormancy has been broken and it will not keep.

Onions are grown by two methods: either from seed, or from small, infant onions called sets. Shallots and garlic are, effectively, grown only from sets, while leeks and spring onions (scallions) are grown from seed. Bunching onions and chives are perennial plants (they live for several years and do not die upon flowering) and may be grown either from seed, division (when the plants are separated to make new plants) or from little bulblets.

GROWING ONIONS FROM SEED

Onions are fairly hardy plants, and small seedlings, growing outdoors, will survive a mild frost. Therefore, seed may be sown outdoors in mid- to late spring, or, with some varieties in mild climates (zones 7–8), in the early autumn.

Sowing onions outside

1 Prepare the ground by removing all weeds, then fork it over and rake it to form a fine tilth and a level surface.

2 Make a drill about 5mm/¼in deep with a thin stick or the corner of the rake head.

3 If the soil is dry, water the bottom of the drill before sowing.

4 Sow the seeds thinly along the bottom. Cover with the soil and firm it lightly with a rake. If sowing on a heavy, clay soil, a thin layer of sharp sand trickled along the bottom of the seed drill will prevent the seed from rotting before it starts to shoot.

5 The seedlings should germinate within 10–15 days. When they are 5–7.5cm/2–3in high, thin them to 7.5–10cm/3–4in apart. Water if conditions are very dry and keep free from weeds.

6 When the seedlings are growing strongly and the leaves are beginning to meet, thin them again to 13–15cm/5–6in apart. The thinnings at this stage of growth may be used as salad or spring onions (scallions). Unless you are intending to grow very large onions, you will not need to thin them again.

7 If you prefer small onions, space them closer together or let them grow as clumps of seedlings – you will then get clumps of small bulbs. Autumn-sown onions are often left to grow as clumps, as they overwinter better than the single seedlings.

Sowing onions indoors

In colder climates or on cold, heavy soils, sow onion seeds indoors under glass and then plant them outside in the garden in late spring. The seeds may be sown in early to mid-spring.

1 Fill a seed tray with sterilized seed compost (growing medium), level the surface and firm it slightly by pressing down gently with your finger.

2 Sprinkle the seed thinly over the surface of the compost.

3 Cover with either a thin layer of sifted seed compost or sprinkle with a thin layer of fine vermiculite to a depth of about 5mm/¼in.

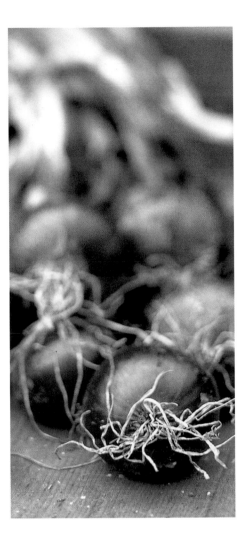

Above: North Holland Blood and Red Mate are both good growing varieties of onions.

4 Using a watering can with a fine rose on the spout, lightly water the seeds, label and cover with a propagator lid or a plastic bag. Gentle heat under the tray will aid germination, but is not essential. As soon as the seedlings begin to emerge, move the tray into full light, but protect the delicate leaves from scorching in strong sunlight.

5 When the seedlings are 5–6cm/2–2½in high, prick them out into trays of compost, spacing them 5–6cm/2–2½in apart.

6 Alternatively, sow the seeds in divided trays or seed modules, 3–4 seeds per module. When the seedlings are growing strongly, thin to one seedling.

Planting onion seedlings outside

Seedlings grown inside will need to be planted outside in late spring. Harden off the seedlings before planting out by standing the trays outside for about 12 days. Cover and protect from heavy rain or frosty weather in a cold frame or greenhouse. When the seedlings have been hardened off, plant out 15–18cm/6–7in apart, in rows 25cm/10in apart. The tiny bulb should be no deeper than it was in the seed tray. Water well and protect from birds.

Some varieties of onion have been specially bred (mainly in Japan) to overwinter in a mild, temperate climate. These should be sown in late summer/early autumn. The seedlings or young plants overwinter, then grow in the spring. These onions are ready for harvesting in the early summer of the year following sowing, and usefully fill the gap between the end of the stored onions and the new season's crop of spring-sown onions. The most famous of these onions are the Vidalia onions, which are grown in the town of the same name in Washington State. The Vidalia onion is famous for being particularly sweet and mild.

GROWING ONIONS FROM SETS

Onions can also be grown from sets, which are small, immature bulbs. Sets have been grown and treated so that, once planted, they will continue to grow to form a full-size onion. Because onions are biennial there is a danger that the set will bolt, that is run to flower, rather than grow to make a fair-size bulb. However, some sets have been heat-treated to kill the flower and prevent bolting. Onion sets are planted in early to mid-spring and will stand a little light frost. They are best planted in open, well-dug soil which has been manured the autumn before planting.

If the soil is heavy, put a little sharp sand beneath each set. Push into the soil in rows, allowing 10cm/4in between sets and 25cm/10in between rows. The top of the set should be just visible. Apart from watering in extremely dry weather and weeding, they should need no more care.

Sometimes birds will work their way down a row pulling out the sets before they have time to root. If this happens, simply push them back into the soil, making sure that they are firm. If birds are proving to be a particular problem, try laying twigs over the soil, or covering the sets with netting. This may well be the best solution to the problem.

Good varieties of onion

Spring sowing: Buffalo, Giant Fen Globe, Ailsa Craig, Sturon, North Holland Blood, Long Red Florence, Red Baron, Southport Red Globe, Red Mate. Autumn sowing: Express Yellow, Imai Early Yellow, Vidalia, Senshyu Yellow. Pickling onions: Paris Silver Skin, Shakespeare.

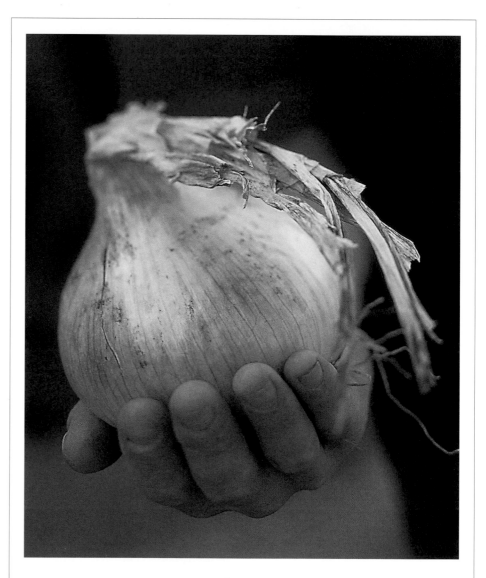

Championship onions and leeks

Around the world, specialist and competitive growers prepare deep beds of special soil in which to grow mammoth onions and leeks. There is great competition between growers. Show leeks are blanched by growing them through drainpipes or wrapping them in thick, corrugated cardboard, and they are fed with "secret" compounds of liquid fertilizer to encourage growth. Some onions can grow to over 2.75kg/6lb, while leeks can grow up to 1m/1yd long, with a stem as thick as a person's arm. Good varieties for championship onions are Mammoth and Beacon.

GROWING LEEKS

Leeks are grown from seed in exactly the same way as onions. Sow outside in mid- to late spring or inside under glass in early spring. Sowing seeds indoors provides a longer growing season and produces bigger leeks. Leeks sown outside should be thinned to about 2.5cm/1in apart. Inside, prick out the seedlings into trays or modules about 2.5cm/1in apart. In early summer, plant the leeks outside. Indoor-sown leeks should be hardened off first.

1 If you want long, blanched leeks, dig a trench of prepared soil. The trench should be about 30cm/12in across and about 25cm/10in deep. Fork over the bottom of the trench thoroughly and dig in some well-rotted manure or fertilizer. Heap the removed soil alongside the trench for infilling later.

2 Half-fill the trench with removed soil, then make holes with a stick or dibber 20–25cm/8–10in apart. They should be about 2.5–4cm/1–1½in across and 13–15cm/5–6in deep.

3 Drop the seedlings into the holes so that the leaves poke out of the top.

4 Water the leeks well, by pouring water into the hole to wash soil over the roots.

5 As the leeks grow, gradually return the remaining soil to the trench. This blanches the stem, and forces the leeks to grow a longer, white stem.

6 For leeks for general cooking, holes may be made in well-prepared soil, rather than a trench. Drop in the leek seedlings and water in as above. Some gardeners on heavy clay soil find they get better results if they grow leeks in raised beds of deeply prepared soil.

Below: De Saint Victor leeks have distinctive blue-purple leaves; they are winter-hardy and have excellent flavour.

This aids drainage, whereas a trench may fill with water on badly draining land. Support the sides with planks of wood, bricks or old railway sleepers (railroad ties). The beds should be about 1.2m/4ft wide so that they can be cultivated without stepping on the soil.

Good varieties of leek

Bleu de Solaise: a handsome leek with blue-purple foliage; Autumn Giant: an early maturing leek that will last to late winter in the ground; Musselborough Improved: a good winter-hardy variety; King Richard: a quick-growing variety, good for harvesting as baby leeks; Jolant; De Saint Victor: winter-hardy.

Fertilizing onions and leeks

In ordinary conditions, onions need little or no feeding during the growing period, although they may be fed with a potash fertilizer when the bulb is well formed. This helps the bulb ripen and prevents it developing "thick neck". Leeks need no extra feeding during the growing season as long as the ground was manured to start with.

GROWING SHALLOTS

Shallots are generally grown from sets rather than from seed. They grow as clumps of bulbs, each one of which may be grown on as a set. They are grown in exactly the same way as onion sets but they grow much more quickly.

1 In late winter to early spring, plant shallot sets in open, well-dug soil that has been well manured the autumn before planting.

2 If the soil is very heavy, place a little sharp sand under every shallot to aid drainage and prevent the bulb from rotting in the wet earth.

3 If any of the sets are pulled up by birds, press them back into the soil. Alternatively, protect the sets with a layer of netting or by laying a few twigs over the soil.

4 The shallots will be ready to harvest by midsummer.

Good varieties of shallot

Atlantic: golden-skinned shallots with a high yield; Pikant: a pink-fleshed shallot of fine flavour; Giant Iona; Topper.

Pests and diseases
The potent chemicals that alliums produce generally give them an in-built defence against pests and diseases. Garlic, in particular, seems resistant to most garden pests.

Rabbits, rodents and deer give all alliums a wide berth because they find the smell and taste offensive. Moles, too, avoid making their runs near an onion or garlic bed. Despite this, mice or rats are known to eat onions in store, so, when alliums are stored, they should be protected against these vermin.

In very wet summers, and on heavy, poorly drained land, onions can be susceptible to downy mildew, which can cause rotting. Affected onions should be pulled up and discarded, but not on the compost heap. Onions should not be grown on the same patch of ground for about three years.

The major pest of onions is onion fly. They lay their eggs in the bulb, which is then eaten by the maggots that hatch from the eggs. There are no chemical treatments that protect onions against this harmful pest, but companion planting is said to be effective in deterring them. Plant tagetes (French marigolds) and parsley in rows among the onions if the pest is known to be prevalent.

Leeks sometimes get a rust disease, which causes rust-coloured spots on the foliage. However, it does not affect the leek stem so there is no need to spray or discard the leek plants, but do not put affected leaves on the compost heap.

Above: Once harvested, shallots are best strung for storage and kept in a dry, frost-free place. They should keep throughout the winter if stored in this way.

GROWING GARLIC

Garlic is grown from individual cloves in a similar way to onion and shallot sets. There are many different varieties of garlic that have been specially bred to suit specific climates. It is better to order an appropriate variety from a seed firm, rather than using a head of garlic from the supermarket as it may have been imported. These will, however, often grow. Garlic needs a long growing season and also a period of 1–2 months of cold weather (0–10°C/32–50°F) to make a good-size head.

Garlic is different from other alliums (apart from the seldom-grown potato onion) in that the head, or bulb, grows underground rather than on the surface of the soil. Because of this, garlic is best planted in the autumn, to be harvested in mid- to late summer the following year. It will tolerate some frost. Little or no growth will be visible above ground until the following spring.

1 Plant individual cloves 10–15cm/ 4–6in apart in rows 25cm/10in apart just below the surface in well-dug soil. Place a little sand beneath each clove if gardening on heavy, clay soil to help drainage and prevent rotting.

Growing garlic shoots

Garlic shoots can easily be grown by planting cloves of garlic in pots of good, free-draining compost (soil mix) from early spring onwards. Keep well watered in a sunny, open position. Harvest the young shoots when they are about 15–20cm/6–8in high. More shoots will soon grow to replace them.

Good varieties of garlic

Moraluz: large white heads; Cristo; Mediterranean.

GROWING SPRING ONIONS

Spring onions (scallions) are grown from seed. Sow as for bulb onions in rows about 20cm/8in apart. Spring onions mature quickly, so sow short rows in succession every 3–4 weeks during spring and early summer. If you sow the seed thinly, there is no need to thin out spring onions, simply pull the onions as you need them.

Good varieties of spring onion

Santa Claus: a Japanese variety with deep-red stems; White Lisbon: a traditional, white, quick-growing spring onion.

GROWING BUNCHING ONIONS

Asian varieties of bunching onions are grown in a similar way to spring onions, but you can keep on harvesting them over a longer period, so thin the plants to about 10cm/4in apart.

Good varieties of bunching onion

Summer Isle; White Evergreen; Ishikura, Kujo Green.

GROWING WELSH ONIONS AND TREE ONIONS

These perennial onions are best bought as small plants from a herb nursery, although it is possible to grow them from seed sown indoors in early spring. If growing from seed, prick out clumps of little seedlings in 7.5-cm/3-in pots. Harden off the seedlings and plant them out in early summer. If you have a mature plant, you can create more by simply digging the plant up and dividing it into smaller plants. Replant small

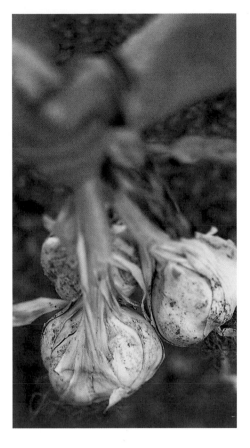

Above: Freshly harvested garlic ready for cleaning and stringing for storage.

sections from the healthy, outer edge of the clumps, rather than from the congested centre. Bulblets from the top of the stem of tree onions will also grow into new plants if pushed into a pot of good compost.

GROWING CHIVES

Chives are propagated by division. They prefer a good, moist soil, but will grow more or less anywhere. Divide the plant when it is actively growing in early or mid-spring and set the divisions about 25cm/10in apart. Chives should be harvested as you need them. During the growing season, they can be cut down to ground level two or three times and they will sprout again, with fresh, full-flavoured leaves. Water well after cutting back. In the autumn, pot up chive plants, cut them back and keep them in a cool, frost-free place indoors where there is plenty of good light. This is a good way to have fresh chives available for use throughout the winter.

HARVESTING AND STORAGE

The harvesting of alliums depends on the length of time that they can be stored. Onions, shallots and garlic, which, if stored correctly, can keep throughout the winter, should be harvested when they are fully grown. Leeks, spring onions (scallions) and chives, which have a shorter shelf life, are better left in the ground until they are needed.

ONIONS, SHALLOTS AND GARLIC

It is obvious when onions, shallots and garlic are ready to be harvested. With onions and shallots, the leaf stem keels over at the top (neck) of the bulb. With garlic, the leaves start to die back, wither and keel over. When this happens, it is fairly certain that the bulb has finished its growth for the season.

Sometimes onions develop a "fat" or "thick" neck. This is not a disease, but a physiological condition. Some varieties are more susceptible than others; wet weather is an additional factor. The neck of the onion becomes thick and remains green, and the leaves do not keel over but stay upright and healthy. The onion still continues to grow, rather than to ripen and dry off. If left in the soil, the onion would eventually bolt, or run to flower. Such onions are perfectly good to eat, but they will not keep for a great length of time, so use them as quickly as possible.

When the onion leaves keel over, it is best to leave them in the soil for a week or so, especially if the weather is dry and sunny. After that, gently pull the onions up to expose the roots to the air and leave them on the ground to finish drying and for the root to wither. If the weather is cold and wet, remove the bulbs to a dry but well-ventilated place: lying on the greenhouse staging is ideal, or on a frame made of netting. Do not remove stems at this time. When the onions have thoroughly dried, the stems may be twisted off and the onions placed in trays with ventilation holes.

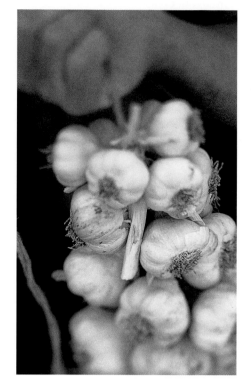

Above: Stringing garlic is an excellent way of making sure that it stays dry and well ventilated.

Left: Lift onions with a fork, then let the bulbs dry off either on the ground, if dry, or on a rack under cover.

Stringing onions, shallots and garlic

If the stems are left intact, the onions may be strung together to form ropes or skeins, either by plaiting (braiding) the stalks or tying them together with string or raffia. Shallots and garlic should be treated in the same way. An alternative method of "stringing" garlic is simply to thread a stiff wire through the dry necks of the bulbs.

Strung onions, shallots and garlic may then be hung up for storage, which is an excellent way of keeping them well aired. All three should keep through to the following spring if stored in a dry, well-ventilated room or shed that is cool and just frost-free. Check your store of onions throughout winter and discard any that feel soft. Towards the end of winter, some onions may begin to sprout. Use these immediately. Do not try to store garlic ropes in the kitchen, however decorative, or they will sprout.

How to string onions, shallots and garlic

Onions, shallots and garlic can all be strung together in the same way. Either tie them into a skein with string or raffia, or plait (braid) the dried stems.

1 Take the first bulb and tie a loop of string around the neck. Pull the string tight to allow for shrinkage later.

2 Add more bulbs, each one just above the last, forming a loop of string around the neck of each. Bind any surplus stem into the skein.

3 When you have reached the end of the skein – usually about 12–15 onions – tie all the stalks together firmly, folding over any surplus.

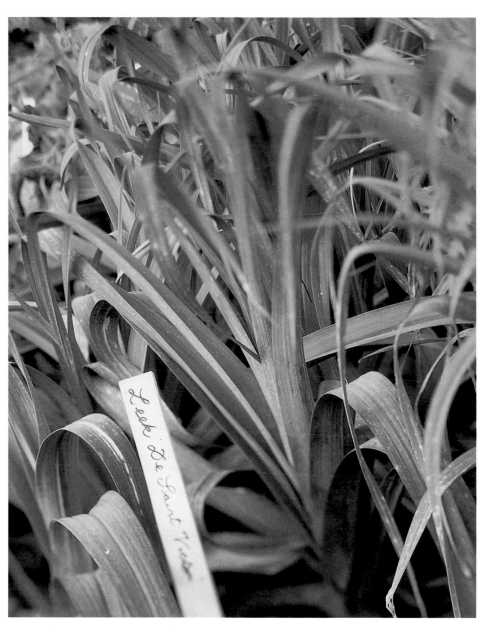

Above: Young leeks, like these 4-month-old De Saint Victors, may be harvested as soon as they begin to thicken.

LEEKS

These are best left in the ground rather than lifting them as they mature. Simply harvest as and when you need them in the kitchen. They will withstand quite hard frosts and can be left in the ground throughout the autumn. When dug, the leeks will keep for about a week in a dry, well-ventilated room. Washed and prepared, leeks should be stored in a plastic bag in the vegetable drawer of the refrigerator.

SPRING ONIONS AND CHIVES

If the spring onions (scallions) have been sown thinly enough then, as they mature, you can simply pull them from the ground when you need them. Once pulled, they should be stored in the refrigerator, wrapped in a plastic bag.

CHIVES

These should not be pulled, but can be snipped near to the soil with a pair of kitchen scissors. Harvest chives as they are required in the kitchen. They will keep for a few days, well-wrapped in a plastic bag or in a plastic tub in the refrigerator.

PREPARING ONIONS AND OTHER ALLIUMS

This section looks at most of the basic techniques for preparing and cooking onions, leeks and other alliums. It is worthwhile spending a little of your time studying and mastering these techniques, since they ultimately help to save time and tears.

CHOOSING ONIONS AND OTHER ALLIUMS

When buying onions, choose firm, undamaged specimens with light skins. Reject any that feel soft when gently squeezed, show signs of dampness or with green shoots at the top. These rules apply to shallots and garlic too, except new season's garlic which should have moist, fresh skins.

Examine the leaves of spring onions (scallions) and leeks – they should be fresh and not brown or slimy. Be careful when buying leeks in late spring and early summer, since they may well have a hard, central core. This core is the developing flower stalk and it will not soften on cooking.

When preparing onions, discard any that have brown patches or are brown or slimy at the centre. The onion will be tainted, and even if the bad portion is cut away and discarded, the onion will still taste nasty.

Green shoots at the centre of a garlic clove, and dried-out, old or withered garlic cloves should be discarded – they will give a bitter or musty taste to the finished dish.

PEELING ONIONS

1 The easiest way to peel an onion is first to cut off the top and bottom.

2 Slit the skin with a sharp knife and peel it off.

Peeling whole onions

Onions or shallots used for braising or for adding to a *boeuf bourguignonne*, for example, must be left whole. Some cooks even find it easier to slice onions, which can be quite slippery and tough, if the root end is temporarily left intact.

1 To peel an onion or shallot, when it is important that the onion stays whole, trim any root from the base, making sure you leave the base intact.

2 Then, working from the neck down, make a shallow slit in the skin from top to bottom with a small, sharp knife.

3 Pull the skin off the onion, working from the neck down.

Peeling small onions and shallots

If you are peeling a lot of small onions or shallots, it is easier if you first blanch them in boiling water. This is particularly helpful when peeling varieties that have tenaciously clinging, tight skins. This also works with garlic cloves.

1 Cut off the neck of the onions or shallots and cut a thin slice off the bottom, but leave the root base intact or the onions may fall apart in cooking.

2 Place in a bowl and add enough boiling water to cover.

3 Leave for about 3 minutes, drain, then slip the onions or shallots out of their skins.

TRIMMING AND CLEANING LEEKS

Particles of soil can easily become trapped in between the leaf layers of a leek. The tighter the layers, the less likelihood there is that soil will have managed to penetrate.

Baby leeks and tight, ready-trimmed leeks from the supermarket are unlikely to be very gritty, but it is still worth checking before cooking, since nothing ruins a leek dish more than the mere trace of grittiness from hidden soil. Leeks fresh from the garden are always the worst culprits and therefore need to be washed thoroughly.

Trimming and cleaning large leeks

1 When preparing large leeks, trim off most of the loose green leaves, or flags, cutting at the point where the layers begin to get tighter.

2 Discard any loose green leaves but, unless the recipe specifies the white part of the leek only, do not discard the green part of the bulb.

3 Trim off excess root. Discard one or two outer layers of the leek, which are tough, fibrous and quite likely to have been damaged.

4 Make a slit starting about 2.5cm/1in from the base of the leek to the top, cutting through to the centre.

5 Carefully wash the leek under cold running water, fanning out the layers with your fingers to make sure you wash away all the dirt. Hold the leek so that the water runs from the base to the top, so dirt will not be washed back into the layers of leaves.

Trimming and cleaning baby leeks

1 Cut off as little of the green leaf as possible, as it is tender enough to eat.

2 Baby leeks are usually clean enough to cook whole, but check one by cutting a slit through to the centre.

3 Peel off the outer layer of the leek if it looks tough or damaged.

4 Wash the leeks by shaking them well in a bowl of cold water.

5 If leeks appear dirty only at the top end and you want to cook the leek whole, cut a short slit in the leek. Either wash the leeks under cold running water or soak them in a bowl of cold, well-salted water for 30 minutes to draw out the dirt. Soaking also leaches out vitamins, so this should be a last resort.

Preparing in advance

It is unwise to prepare any of the onion family too far in advance. Raw alliums can develop "off-flavours" as a result of the sulphur compounds that are released when their cell walls are broken. Although safe to eat, they can taint delicate dishes of eggs, cream and butter. If you want to prepare alliums ahead of time, cook them briefly in a little fat from the recipe (or blanch them in boiling water for a few minutes).

SLICING AND CHOPPING ONIONS, SHALLOTS AND LEEKS

1 The easiest way to slice an onion is to cut it in half with a sharp knife, from neck to root.

2 Place the halves, cut sides down, on the chopping board.

3 Hold down one half firmly, but tuck your fingertips in, away from the blade of the knife, then, using the knuckles to guide the knife blade, cut down to make slices. Repeat with the other half.

Cutting crescent-shaped slices

Crescent-shaped slices of onion are good in salads and stir-fries. Thicker wedges are excellent for roasting.

1 Leave the root end of the onion intact and cut the bulb in half vertically, from neck to root.

2 Lay the onion, cut side down, on a board and, using a sharp knife, cut thin slices following the curve of the onion.

3 Leave these thin slices attached at the base for frying or separate them into layers for salad garnishes.

Cutting onion rings

1 Choose evenly shaped round onions. Look at the neck of the bulb and check that there is only one shoot, or neck – this means that there is more chance of getting perfectly round onion rings.

2 Cut a thin slice from one side so that it will not slip on the chopping board.

3 Cut down to form thin or thick slices. Push out to separate into rings.

Chopping onions

1 Slice the onion in half from top to bottom and lay it cut side down.

2 Slice across the onion, leaving a small section uncut at the root end.

3 Slice down through the onion at right angles to these cuts from neck to root. Leave the root end uncut to prevent the onion falling apart.

4 Finally, slice across the onion at right angles to the second set of cuts and the onion will fall into dice on the chopping board as you cut.

Slicing leeks

1 Cut across the width of the leek in the thickness you require.

COOK'S TIP

The green part of the leek often takes a little longer to cook than the tender white part, so put it into the pan a few minutes earlier.

2 When stir-frying, cut across the leek obliquely in a series of diagonal cuts. This exposes a larger surface area of the central portion of the leek to the heat, so that it cooks quickly.

Chopping leeks

1 Using a sharp knife, carefully cut the leek in half vertically, from top to root. Lay the leek, cut side down, on the chopping board.

2 Make a series of cuts along the length of the leek from bottom to top, leaving the root end intact to prevent the leek from falling apart.

3 Cut across the leek and it will fall into dice on the chopping board.

PREPARING SPRING ONIONS AND BUNCHING ONIONS

Spring onions (scallions) and bunching onions are easily prepared. Cut off only tough or damaged green leaves. Peel the thin, outer layer from the onion and trim the root end. Wash in a bowl of cold water or under running water. For stir-frying, simply slice at an oblique angle, holding the knife blade at about 40 degrees to the length of the onion.

Spring onion brushes

These are traditionally served with Peking duck. The fringed end of the onion may be used to dip into the plum sauce for brushing it on to the pancakes.

1 Cut the spring onion into 6–7.5cm/ 2½–3in lengths.

2 Make a series of lengthways cuts at one end of the spring onion, using a sharp knife or kitchen scissors to produce a tassel effect. Leave at least half the onion uncut to form a handle.

3 Place the spring onions in a bowl of iced water and chill in the refrigerator for 30–45 minutes to allow them to curl.

Making spring onion curls

1 Cut the spring onion into 6–7.5cm/ 2½–3in lengths.

2 Cut each piece in half lengthways, then cut these pieces lengthways into long, thin shreds.

3 Place in a bowl of iced water and chill in the refrigerator for 30 minutes to allow the shreds to curl.

Making spring onion tassels

1 Make a series of short, lengthways cuts at each end of the onions using a sharp knife or kitchen scissors to produce a tassel effect. Make sure you leave at least 2.5cm/1in of onion uncut at the centre.

2 Chill the spring onions in iced water for 30–45 minutes until the ends curl.

CUTTING CHIVES

1 Hold a bunch of chives in your hand, snip the bunch level at one end with kitchen scissors, then snip off the amount you require.

2 Cut straight across to form little rings, or obliquely to form slanting chives.

PREPARING GARLIC

The taste of garlic differs depending on how it is prepared. This is because varying amounts of the natural sulphur compounds, which are contained in garlic, are released depending on how you cut it. The finer you chop or crush garlic, the stronger the flavour will be.

Peeling garlic

The easiest way to peel garlic is to place it on a chopping board and use the blade of a wide-bladed knife flat to crush the clove.

1 Lay the blade of a knife flat on the clove and press down firmly on the blade with your fist or the heel of your hand, breaking the skin of the garlic.

2 The skin will then peel off easily. This also bruises the garlic, which allows the flavour to come out.

COOK'S TIP

To remove the smell of garlic from your hands, sprinkle them with salt, then rinse in cold water before washing them with hot water and soap. Alternatively, rub them all over with the cut side of a lemon before washing in hot water.

Blanching garlic

If peeling a lot of garlic, you can blanch the cloves to make them easier to peel.

1 Cut off the top and bottom of each garlic clove and place in a bowl of boiling water for 2–3 minutes. Drain, then slip the cloves out of their skins.

Chopping garlic

1 When chopping or crushing garlic, first remove any green shoot at the centre of the cloves. The shoot is most apparent in late winter/spring and can taste bitter. Cut out the shoot with the tip of a knife or pinch it out.

2 For a mild flavour, slice garlic thinly, across the clove, or chop coarsely.

3 For a stronger flavour, finely chop the garlic by first cutting the clove in half from top to bottom, then cutting along and then across the clove.

Crushing garlic

To attain a much stronger flavour, crush the garlic rather than chopping it.

1 Crush the garlic in a mortar with a pestle or, alternatively, crush it on a chopping board with the flat blade of a knife to make a paste. Adding a few flakes of sea salt to the garlic will make crushing much easier.

2 Easier still, press the peeled clove through a specially designed garlic press or crusher.

GARLIC GADGETS

The only tools you really need to prepare garlic are a good, small, sharp knife, a chopping board and, of course, your hands. However, there are plenty of pieces of equipment on the market that are designed to help with the preparation of garlic. Most of this equipment has just one aim in mind – to minimize handling the garlic and therefore preventing the hands from smelling of it.

Garlic peeler

Garlic peelers are made of a simple rubber tube with a textured inside surface. The garlic clove is placed inside the tube, which is then pressed down on and rolled back and forth on the work surface to loosen the skin for easier peeling.

Garlic press (pump action)

A pump action garlic press is the most familiar type of garlic crusher. Some presses have a very useful reverse action that helps to extract the garlic that can become trapped in the holes. Garlic presses can also be used for preparing onion and ginger juice.

Garlic press (screw action)

A different type of press from the pump action, but the result is basically the same. As you screw down the handle, the garlic is pressed out of the head. It is easy to use, but not so easy to clean.

Mortar and pestle

These are very useful pieces of general kitchen equipment and are excellent for crushing large quantities of garlic or making garlicky pastes, such as aioli.

Below: A mortar and pestle are the traditional devices for crushing garlic.

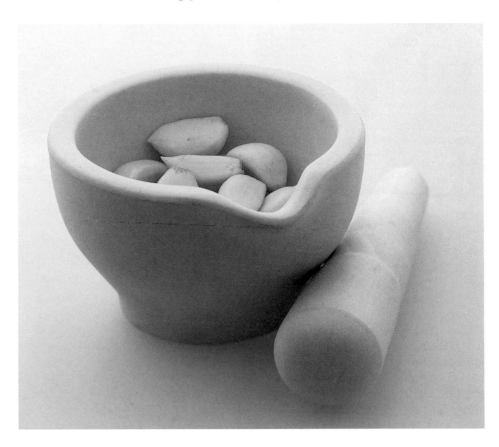

Garlic crush

A garlic crush is similar to a pestle but has a larger domed base. It is most effective when used with a bowl-shaped board. It produces a similar result to garlic crushed with the flat blade of a large knife.

Garlic slicer

A garlic slicer acts like a miniature mandolin. The garlic clove is placed in the holder, then slid back and forth over the sharp blade. This gadget is particularly useful if you are slicing large quantities of garlic or ginger.

COOKING ONIONS AND OTHER ALLIUMS

There are many ways of cooking onions, all of which will produce very different results both in the flavour of the onion and in the dish in which it is used.

FRYING ONIONS

Onions can be fried in a number of different ways and each gives its own unique result. Onions that are quickly fried until they are brown will retain all the pungency of the raw onion and may taste quite bitter if allowed to get too brown. Quick-fried onions are generally used in dishes where they will receive further cooking, such as stews and casseroles – dishes that also benefit from the dark colour the browned onions impart to the sauce.

Slow-cooked onions, cooked over a low heat in a covered pan and not allowed to brown at all, will develop a wonderful, mellow, sweet taste that can add a great depth of flavour to the finished dish. This process is called sweating, and is an essential first step in preparing many soups and sauces. It works well with leeks, too.

Caramelizing onions is a combination of these two methods. First the onions are cooked slowly until soft but not browned, then the heat is turned up and the onions are cooked uncovered until they brown. In some recipes, a little sugar is added to speed up the caramelizing process. When the onions are cooked slowly to a mahogany brown, they are used as the base of many rich, brown soups and many classic sauces. They are also good to eat just as they are as an accompaniment to meat, poultry or cheese.

Different kinds of onion, or onions at different stages of growth, react in different ways to these basic cooking techniques. Green, unripened onions will not fry to a dry crispness. Red onions tend to be "wetter" than yellow Spanish (Bermuda) onions and so they tend not to brown and caramelize so easily. Shallots are quite dry-fleshed and will soon dry out and turn bitter and hard if they are fried and browned too quickly. To keep onions soft and prevent them from browning when frying, add a pinch of salt to draw out their moisture.

Quick frying

1 Heat whatever fat the recipe calls for in a large, heavy frying pan over a medium heat until hot. Add the thinly sliced or chopped onions and cook for about 5 minutes, stirring frequently to prevent them from sticking to the pan, until the onions begin to turn brown at the edges. Do not allow to burn as this will spoil the flavour.

Slow frying

1 Cook the onions over a very low heat for 10–15 minutes, until they collapse and turn a deep golden yellow colour. Stir the onions occasionally while they cook to prevent them from sticking to the pan and browning, as this will spoil their mellow flavour.

Sweating

This cooking process can be used for onions or leeks and is often the first step in soup making, as it concentrates and mellows the flavour, producing a rounder taste. Sweating or slow-frying requires a very low heat that cooks, but does not brown the onions or leeks, as this destroys the mellow, sweet flavour.

1 Cook the onions as for shallow frying, but cover the pan with a lid to produce a much softer, sweeter result.

2 Some cooks like to press a piece of greaseproof (waxed) paper or baking parchment on top of the onions before covering them with the lid. This sweats the onions even more intensely.

Remedies for onion odours
• Try rubbing the soles of your feet with pure peppermint oil. Within 30 minutes the smell on your breath should be of mint.
• Chewing fresh parsley is the best-known antidote to onions and garlic on the breath. The chlorophyll in the parsley neutralizes the sulphur chemicals released by the alliums, which cause odours.
• Cover over the onion smells by chewing cardamom or fennel seeds – these seeds are traditionally offered after Indian meals as breath fresheners and an aid to digestion.
• Drink a herbal infusion or tea of mint, fennel and/or sage.

Thai crisp-fried shallots

These are excellent for garnishing salads, rice and soups.

1 Peel the shallots and slice to a medium thickness.

2 Cook the shallots gently in oil for about 8 minutes, until they soften.

3 Raise the heat and fry the shallots briskly until they brown and crisp. Remove with a slotted spoon and drain well on kitchen paper.

COOK'S TIP
Dried shallot or onion slices can be fried from dry to form a crisp-fried garnish. Take care not to burn them.

CARAMELIZING

To caramelize onions or shallots, they need to be cooked slowly until their natural sugars turn an appetizing brown colour. Caramelized onions or shallots add a depth of flavour to soups, sauces and stews. They are also good served with liver, steak or sausages.

The speed with which onions will caramelize depends on the heat of the pan. Onions or shallots caramelized over a very low heat for 45 minutes will slowly turn a deep mahogany brown. The cooking time will depend on the onions' sugar content. Caramelized onions are used most famously in *soupe à l'oignon*. For a quicker result, raise the heat and add just a little sugar to aid caramelization, but stir frequently to prevent the onions from sticking.

Caramelizing onions in a pan

1 Cook onions slowly, covered, in butter or oil until they soften and turn golden.

2 Continue cooking, uncovered, until they begin to brown at the edges, stirring them frequently.

3 Add 2.5–5ml/½–1 tsp sugar to help the onions to caramelize more quickly.

Caramelizing onions in the oven

This technique can be quite useful if you are busy, because the onions do not need to be stirred quite so often as onions caramelized in a pan.

1 Place thickly sliced onions in a roasting pan or on a baking tray, season with salt and pepper to taste, add herbs, such as thyme or rosemary, and sprinkle with a little olive oil.

2 Cover the onions with foil and cook at 190°C/375°F/Gas 5 for 30 minutes.

3 Uncover the pan or tray, stir in 5ml/1 tsp sugar and sprinkle a little wine or balsamic vinegar over the onions.

4 Return the pan or tray to the oven, uncovered this time, and cook for another 25–35 minutes, stirring once or twice, by which time the onions should be very soft and browned.

COOK'S TIP
A thick layer of onions will caramelize better than a thin layer, which will brown too quickly. Keep an eye on them in the oven. If they brown too quickly, lower the heat and be sure to stir once or twice.

Caramelizing shallots or baby onions

Shallots and baby (pearl) onions are usually caramelized whole, but they can also be cooked in thick slices.

1 Brown the shallots or baby onions lightly on all sides in a little butter or oil. Raise the heat slightly, sprinkle in a little sugar, then cook the shallots until the sugar begins to caramelize.

2 Add seasoning, herbs, if using, and a fairly shallow layer of a liquid to suit the recipe, such as wine, stock or vinegar. Cook gently, covered, until the shallots or onions are tender but still whole.

3 Then cook, uncovered, at a higher heat, until all the liquid has evaporated.

FRYING GARLIC

Because of garlic's relatively low moisture content, it fries and browns more quickly than onions. It will burn easily and develops a bitter, acrid taste. Therefore, when a recipe calls for onions and garlic to be fried together, add the garlic to the pan when the onions are almost cooked.

In Chinese and Asian cooking, garlic is often fried in oil at the beginning of cooking. Sometimes it is removed and discarded afterwards because only the flavoured oil is wanted in the dish; at other times, the garlic is an integral part of the dish. Again, care needs to be taken that the garlic cooks to an even, light brown, when it has a delicious toasty flavour.

Frying garlic slices

1 Heat a wok or deep frying pan until hot, add some cooking oil and allow it to become hot.

2 Add finely sliced garlic to the wok or pan and immediately stir it through the oil. It will begin to colour at once.

3 Remove the garlic with a slotted spoon as soon as it is a light brown.

Frying whole garlic cloves

Fried cloves of garlic make a delicious addition to green salads, especially those with goat's cheese.

1 Choose large, plump garlic cloves and peel them. Bring a large pan of water to the boil and throw in the garlic, cook for 3–4 minutes, then drain.

2 Repeat the blanching process, then drain and dry thoroughly.

3 Heat a shallow layer of oil in a wok or frying pan, then fry the garlic gently until it turns an even, medium brown.

4 Remove with a slotted spoon and drain well on kitchen paper.

GRILLING

Cooking onions, leeks and spring onions (scallions) in this way gives a delicious result. They are perfect for serving as an accompaniment. Grilling (broiling) – either under a grill (broiler), over hot coals or using a griddle pan – gives onions, leeks and spring onions a sweet, mellow flavour.

Grilling onions

Onions, particularly mild, sweet onions, grill very successfully and are especially good when cooked over hot coals.

1 Peel the onions and slice them horizontally into thick slices, discarding the thin slices from the top and bottom of the onion. Carefully spear the slices on an oiled metal skewer, passing the skewer through the slices so that all the layers are kept flat.

2 Brush the skewered onion slices with oil, season, then grill for 5–6 minutes on each side or until the onions are soft and slightly charred.

3 Alternatively, place the onion slices in a grill cage, brush with oil and season, then grill each side for 5–6 minutes.

Grilling spring onions

Spring onions are delicious grilled and are very good as an accompaniment to grilled fish, poultry and meat dishes or served with cheese. They are very popular in Mexico and Cataluña where they are known as *calçots* and eaten with a spicy chilli sauce.

1 Choose big, fat spring onions with large bulbs for grilling.

2 Trim off any damaged leaves and the outer skin; trim off the root, too, but leave the end intact.

3 Brush with a little oil and grill, either over charcoal on a barbecue or on a cast-iron, ridged grill pan, for about 2 minutes each side, or until softened and browned but not too charred. In Cataluña the outer skin is often peeled off before eating.

COOK'S TIP
Whole grilled cipolla onions make unusual and delicious canapés. After cooking, marinate the grilled cipolla onions in French dressing and serve on rounds of toasted bread or simply with thick slices of fresh crusty bread.

Grilling leeks

Baby leeks, when very small, may be grilled in a similar way to spring onions. However, leeks are usually blanched for a few minutes in boiling water before grilling, since they have tougher skins than spring onions.

1 Bring a large pan of lightly salted water to the boil and throw in the trimmed leeks. Cook baby leeks for 2–3 minutes and cook larger leeks for 4–5 minutes, then drain.

2 Cool a little, then gently squeeze the excess water out of the leeks. Leave baby leeks whole. Cut large leeks in half lengthways or into short logs. Dry on a clean dishtowel or kitchen paper.

3 Brush the leeks with oil, season with salt and pepper to taste, then grill baby leeks as for spring onions, allowing 3–4 minutes each side. Grill large leeks for about 4–5 minutes each side.

COOK'S TIP
Grilled leeks may be served hot, warm or cold. They are particularly delicious with a simple dressing of oil, tarragon vinegar and a little mustard.

ROASTING ONIONS

Onions are delicious roasted. They can be roasted in their skins, which will produce a soft, juicy, sweet centre, or they can be peeled, which produces a more caramelized taste and a much crisper texture.

Roasting onions in their skins

1   Remove any damaged skin and cut off excess root, leaving the base intact.

2   Brush with oil if you like, then roast at 190°C/375°F/Gas 5 until they feel soft when gently squeezed (1–1½ hours).

3   To serve, cut a cross in the top and add butter or cheese. A flavoured butter with herbs or chilli is especially good.

Roasting peeled onions

1   Small, peeled onions may be roasted whole. Larger onions may be cut into wedges (leaving them attached at the root base, so they don't fall apart on cooking) or, alternatively, they can be cut into halves or quarters.

2   Alternatively, make 2–3 cross-cuts from the top down to 1cm/½in from the root base. As they roast, the layers of the onion will open out.

3   Whole onions will roast more quickly if first blanched in boiling water for 3–4 minutes. Toss in oil, season, and cook, uncovered at 190–200°C/375–400°F/Gas 5–6. Whole onions take 40 minutes; wedges about 30 minutes.

STUFFING ONIONS

Onions make natural containers for stuffings, and these may be prepared in two ways.

Preparing raw onion cups for stuffing

1   Choose round, even-shaped onions, not flat or pointed onions. Large Spanish (Bermuda) onions are best.

2   Peel and cut a thin slice off each end so that the cups will stay upright.

3   Using a sharp knife, cut the onion in half horizontally.

4   Using a sharp, pointed knife, cut round the second or third layer of onion, counting in from the outer layer.

5 Gradually loosen the centre of the onion from the outer layers, leaving a cup of two or three layers.

6 If any of the cups has a hole in the base, cover it with a small piece of the removed onion. Fill with stuffing and cook according to the recipe.

To prepare whole onions for stuffing

Whole onions need to be blanched first so that they will cook evenly. The flesh can then be scooped out and mixed with the stuffing. Allow one large onion per person.

1 Choose round, even-shaped onions, peel, but leave the top and especially the root base intact.

2 Cover in lightly salted, boiling water and cook for 15 minutes, then drain thoroughly and set aside until cool enough to handle.

3 Cut off and remove a cap from the top of the onion.

4 Using a small, sharp knife and a pointed or serrated teaspoon, remove the centre of the onion to leave a shell two or three layers thick.

Making stuffing

The most popular stuffings for onions are either meat, or breadcrumbs with herbs, spices and cheese. The stuffing usually incorporates the chopped onion that has been removed.

Raw onion cups are best suited to meaty fillings as they need cooking for 1–1½ hours at 180–190°C/350–375°F/Gas 4–5. They cook best if sat on a bed of sauce or a mixture of olive oil and lemon juice, so that the onions may be basted while they cook. This helps to stop them drying out and keeps them moist. Blanched, partially cooked whole onions should be brushed with a little oil or melted butter and baked for 45–60 minutes.

Watering eyes

Peeling and chopping onions makes you cry because these actions release the volatile chemicals that give onions their strength and bite. They travel to the eyes and nasal cavities through the water vapour in juicy onions. The stronger and juicier the onion, the more it will make you cry. Shallots and garlic, although often containing more of the offending allicins, contain less water, so produce less vapour and hence fewer tears. Leeks are very mild and hardly ever cause tears during preparation.

Most cures for onion tears have to be taken with a pinch of salt, but here are a few that people claim help.

• Chilling an onion for several hours in the refrigerator (or the freezer for a few minutes) is said to "lock-in" the water vapour and prevent it from reaching your eyes.

• Peeling onions under water will prevent the water vapour reaching your nose and eyes, but no one's suggesting you try chopping onions underwater!

• The chemicals mostly reach your tear ducts through your nose, so try breathing through your mouth rather than your nose.

• If you are preparing a lot of small onions, try peeling them by the blanching method – this reduces the chemical spray that's released when onions are peeled.

• When preparing onions, try leaving the base (root) end intact, or cut it last of all. This basal portion of the onion contains the highest concentration of tear-causing allicins.

• An old wives' tale suggests that if you bite on a crust of bread while preparing onions, then you won't cry. Maybe the crust forms a barrier to prevent the onion's water vapour from reaching your nose and eyes.

PICKLING AND PRESERVING

Once, pickling was an important way of storing vegetables through the lean winter months, but nowadays onions are pickled because people like the taste. Although onions, shallots and garlic keep well in their natural state, pickling has always been a popular way of keeping them because their naturally strong flavour survives the pickling process so well and stands up to the strong tastes of vinegar and spices.

Pickling onions

Choose small, firm even-shaped onions for pickling and peel them by the blanching method. Onions to be pickled are usually salted to remove water and to make sure they keep well.

For crisp pickled onions, cover with cold vinegar. For a softer pickle, the onions may be cooked in the hot vinegar for up to 10 minutes.

1 The onions can be layered with sea salt in a non-reactive (i.e. non-metallic) bowl.

2 Alternatively, put the onions in a bowl and cover with a strong brine solution. Set aside to soak.

3 Weight the onions to make sure that they are covered by the brine.

4 After 1–2 days in the brine (this depends on the size of the onions), the onions should be rinsed and patted dry, then packed into clean, sterilized jars.

5 Pour spiced vinegar over the onions.

6 Extra spices can be added to the jar if you like, then tightly seal the jars for storage.

COOK'S TIP
Spices, which can be added for extra flavouring, may include mustard seeds, peppercorns, coriander seeds, allspice, chillies and cloves.

Simple spiced vinegar
Heat together 1.2 litres/2 pints/5 cups vinegar (light or dark malt has the best keeping qualities) with 2 pieces of dried ginger root, 2 blades of mace, 2–3 dried red chillies and 15ml/1 tbsp each mustard seeds, coriander seeds and black peppercorns. Add a few bay leaves, a piece of cinnamon stick or 2–3 star anise to taste. The longer you heat the flavourings with the vinegar, the stronger the taste will become. For a sweeter vinegar, dissolve 45ml/3 tbsp of muscovado (molasses) sugar in the vinegar.

To sterilize jars

Wash, rinse and dry thoroughly. Heat the oven to 180°C/350°F/Gas 4. Making sure you remove any rubber seals first, place the jars on a tray, then heat the jars for about 20 minutes. Cool a little before handling them – the jars will be very hot.

Jars can also be sterilized by putting them in a pan of boiling water for 10 minutes. Stand them on a trivet so that they are not directly over the heat.

OTHER WAYS OF PRESERVING ALLIUMS

Drying onions

In the past, drying was a popular way of preserving onions, but it is less so now, since onions are available fresh all year round. However, dried onions can make a useful store-cupboard (pantry) ingredient for emergencies. To use dried onions, add them directly to stews or casseroles, or reconstitute them in a little warm water for 10–15 minutes first. Dried shallots may be fried in a little oil over a medium heat to produce excellent crisp-fried shallots, which are useful as a garnish for many Thai and South-east Asian dishes.

1 Peel and thinly slice the onions, then lay them on racks.

2 Leave them in a very low oven (110°C/225°F/Gas ¼) until very dry. This will take anything up to 12 hours. Turn the slices once as they dry.

3 Store the onions in a cloth or paper bag in a dry place or in a jar with a cloth or paper lid to absorb any residual moisture. Shallots may be dried in the same way.

Making roasted garlic purée

This makes a very useful flavouring to have in the refrigerator. It will store for several weeks as long as you keep the purée covered with at least 1cm/½in of oil. Top up the oil when you remove some purée. As a guide, one head of garlic will yield about 15–30ml/1–2 tbsp of purée.

The purée is useful in many dishes. To make a simple sauce for pasta, stir 2–3 tbsp of the purée into 150ml/¼ pint/⅔ cup of heated, bubbling double (heavy) cream, season with salt and pepper to taste and add a little lemon juice and some chopped thyme or basil. This is good with many vegetarian dishes too. The purée is also good in soufflés, omelettes and tarts, or simply spread on good bread and eaten with some grilled (broiled) or baked goat's cheese.

Roasted garlic purée

The following quantities make 120ml/4fl oz/½ cup purée.

5 large heads garlic
2–3 sprigs thyme or rosemary
  or both
extra virgin olive oil
salt and ground black pepper

COOK'S TIP

When puréeing this amount of garlic, it is easier to purée the garlic, skins and all, in a food mill or mouli legumes. The mill will force through the soft garlic, leaving all the papery skins and debris behind.

Using a dehydrator

If you are planning on drying a lot of onions, it may be worthwhile for you to invest in a domestic dehydrator. They are easy to use and will enable you to dry large quantities of onions quickly and efficiently. They are also useful for drying other vegetables and fruit, as well as being handy for quick-drying fresh herbs. Follow the manufacturer's instructions for timing.

1 Cut a thin slice off the top of each head of garlic.

2 Wrap the garlic heads in foil with the herbs and drizzle over 45ml/3 tbsp oil. Bake at 190°C/375°F/Gas 5 for 50–60 minutes, or until the garlic is soft, then cool.

3 Squeeze the garlic out of its skin into a bowl, then mash, beat in the oil and season.

4 Spoon into a sterilized jar. Pour over oil to cover by about 1cm/½in. Cover and store in the refrigerator for up to 3 weeks.

Freezing

It is not recommended to freeze raw alliums, since they can develop "off-flavours" because of the sulphur compounds that are released when they are cut. Sauces that contain raw garlic or onion should also be frozen with caution. With pesto, for instance, prepare and freeze the basil, pine nut and oil paste and add the garlic and grated cheeses only on thawing.

We add onions to marinades, to stews and casseroles, to roasts and braises, and we give them a starring role in soups, flans and baked dishes. Certain classics stand out: French Onion Soup with Gruyère Croûtes, Onion Tart, Jansson's Temptation and Lamb Smothered in Onions and North African Spices. Try to imagine a Spanish tortilla or a dish of Italian pasta without onions — it doesn't bear thinking about. In fact, it is hard to think of many savoury recipes in which onions aren't an essential ingredient.

Onion Dishes

FRENCH ONION SOUP
WITH GRUYÈRE CROÛTES

THIS IS PERHAPS THE MOST FAMOUS OF ALL ONION SOUPS. TRADITIONALLY, IT WAS SERVED AS A SUSTAINING EARLY MORNING MEAL TO THE PORTERS AND WORKERS OF LES HALLES MARKET IN PARIS.

SERVES SIX

INGREDIENTS
    50g/2oz/¼ cup butter
    15ml/1 tbsp olive oil
    2kg/4½lb yellow onions, peeled
        and sliced
    5ml/1 tsp chopped fresh thyme
    5ml/1 tsp caster (superfine) sugar
    15ml/1 tbsp sherry vinegar
    1.5 litres/2½ pints/6¼ cups good
        beef, chicken or duck stock
    25ml/1½ tbsp plain (all-
        purpose) flour
    150ml/¼ pint/⅔ cup dry white wine
    45ml/3 tbsp brandy
    salt and ground black pepper
For the croûtes
    6–12 thick slices day-old French
        stick, about 2.5cm/1in thick
    1 garlic clove, halved
    15ml/1 tbsp French mustard
    115g/4oz/1 cup coarsely grated
        Gruyère cheese

1 Melt the butter with the oil in a large pan. Add the onions and stir to coat them in the fat. Cook over a medium heat for 5–8 minutes, stirring once or twice, until the onions begin to soften. Stir in the thyme.

2 Reduce the heat to very low, cover the pan and cook the onions for 20–30 minutes, stirring frequently, until they are very soft and golden yellow.

3 Uncover the pan and increase the heat slightly. Stir in the sugar and cook for 5–10 minutes, until the onions start to brown. Add the sherry vinegar and increase the heat again, then continue cooking, stirring frequently, until the onions turn a deep, golden brown – this could take up to 20 minutes.

COOK'S TIP
The long slow cooking of the onions is the key to success with this soup. If the onions brown too quickly, the soup will be bitter.

4 Meanwhile, bring the stock to the boil in another pan. Stir the flour into the onions and cook for about 2 minutes, then gradually pour in the hot stock. Add the wine and brandy and season the soup to taste with salt and pepper. Simmer for 10–15 minutes.

5 For the croûtes, preheat the oven to 150°C/300°F/Gas 2. Place the slices of bread on a greased baking tray and bake for 15–20 minutes, until dry and lightly browned. Rub the bread with the cut surface of the garlic and spread with the mustard, then sprinkle the grated Gruyère cheese over the slices.

6 Preheat the grill (broiler) on the hottest setting. Ladle the soup into a large flameproof pan or six flameproof bowls. Float the croûtes on the soup, then grill (broil) until the cheese melts, bubbles and browns. Serve immediately.

CEVICHE WITH RED ONION, AVOCADO AND SWEET POTATO

CEVICHE IS A SOUTH AMERICAN DISH OF FISH MARINATED IN CITRUS JUICE AND ONION, WHICH HAS A SIMILAR EFFECT TO COOKING, MAKING THE FISH OPAQUE AND FIRM IN TEXTURE.

SERVES SIX AS AN APPETIZER

INGREDIENTS

675g/1½lb white fish fillets, skinned
1 red onion, thinly sliced
pinch of dried red chilli flakes
grated rind of 1 small lime and
 juice of 5 limes
450–500g/1–1¼lb sweet potatoes
75ml/5 tbsp mild olive oil
15–25ml/3–5 tsp rice vinegar
2.5–5ml/½–1 tsp caster
 (superfine) sugar
2.5 ml/½ tsp ground toasted
 cumin seeds
½–1 fresh red or green chilli, seeded
 and finely chopped
1 large or 2 small avocados, peeled,
 stoned (pitted) and sliced
225g/8oz peeled cooked prawns
 (shrimp)
45ml/3 tbsp chopped fresh
 coriander (cilantro)
30ml/2 tbsp roasted peanuts, chopped
salt and ground black pepper

1 Cut the fish into strips or chunks. Sprinkle half the onion over the base of a glass dish and lay the fish on top. Sprinkle on the dried red chilli flakes and pour in the lime juice. Cover and chill for 2–3 hours, spooning the lime juice over the fish once or twice. Drain, and discard the onion.

2 Steam or boil the sweet potatoes for 20–25 minutes, or until just tender. Peel and slice, or cut into wedges.

3 Place the oil in a bowl and whisk in the rice vinegar and sugar to taste, then add the cumin, season and whisk in the fresh chilli and grated lime rind.

4 In a glass bowl, toss together the fish, sweet potatoes, avocado slices, prawns and most of the coriander, and the dressing.

5 Toss in the remaining half of the sliced red onion. Sprinkle with the remaining coriander and the peanuts and serve immediately.

COOK'S TIP
Choose orange-fleshed sweet potatoes if you can for this dish.

POTATO AND ONION TORTILLA WITH BROAD BEANS

THE CLASSIC TORTILLA OR SPANISH OMELETTE INCLUDES NOTHING MORE THAN ONIONS, POTATO, EGGS AND OLIVE OIL. ADDING CHOPPED HERBS AND A FEW SKINNED BROAD BEANS MAKES THIS A VERY SUMMERY DISH TO ENJOY AT LUNCH, OR CUT IT INTO SMALL PIECES AND SERVE AS A SPANISH TAPAS.

SERVES TWO

INGREDIENTS
 45ml/3 tbsp olive oil
 2 Spanish (Bermuda) onions,
  thinly sliced
 300g/11oz waxy potatoes, cut into
  1cm/½in dice
 250g/9oz/1¾ cups shelled broad
  (fava) beans
 5ml/1 tsp chopped fresh thyme
 6 large (US extra large) eggs
 45ml/3 tbsp mixed chopped chives
  and chopped flat leaf parsley
 salt and ground black pepper

1 Heat 30ml/2 tbsp of the oil in a 23cm/9in deep non-stick frying pan. Add the onions and potatoes and stir to coat. Cover and cook gently, stirring frequently, for 20–25 minutes, until the potatoes are cooked and the onions collapsed. Do not let the mixture brown.

2 Meanwhile, cook the beans in boiling salted water for 5 minutes. Drain well and set aside to cool.

3 When the beans are cool enough to handle, peel off the grey outer skins. Add the beans to the frying pan, together with the chopped thyme and season with salt and pepper to taste. Stir well to mix and cook for a further 2–3 minutes.

4 Beat the eggs with salt and pepper to taste and the mixed herbs, then pour the mixture over the potatoes and onions and increase the heat slightly. Cook gently until the egg on the bottom sets and browns, gently pulling the omelette away from the sides of the pan and tilting it to allow the uncooked egg to run underneath.

5 Invert the tortilla on to a plate. Add the remaining oil to the pan and heat until hot. Slip the tortilla back into the pan, uncooked side down, and cook for another 3–5 minutes to allow the underneath to brown. Slide the tortilla out on to a plate. Divide as you like, and serve warm rather than piping hot.

SPICED ONION KOFTAS

THESE DELICIOUS INDIAN ONION FRITTERS ARE MADE WITH CHICKPEA FLOUR, OTHERWISE KNOWN AS GRAM FLOUR OR BESAN. SERVE WITH CHUTNEY OR YOGURT DIP.

SERVES FOUR TO FIVE

INGREDIENTS
675g/1½lb onions, halved and
thinly sliced
5ml/1 tsp salt
5ml/1 tsp ground coriander
5ml/1 tsp ground cumin
2.5ml/½ tsp ground turmeric
1–2 green chillies, seeded and
finely chopped
45ml/3 tbsp chopped fresh
coriander (cilantro)
90g/3½oz/¾ cup chickpea flour
2.5ml/½ tsp baking powder
vegetable oil, for deep-frying
To serve
lemon wedges (optional)
fresh coriander (cilantro) sprigs
yogurt and herb dip or yogurt and
cucumber dip

1 Place the onions in a colander, add the salt and toss. Place on a plate and leave to stand for 45 minutes, tossing once or twice. Rinse the onions, then squeeze out any excess moisture.

2 Place the onions in a bowl. Add the ground coriander, cumin, turmeric, chillies and fresh coriander. Mix well.

COOK'S TIPS
• To make a yogurt and herb dip, stir 30ml/2 tbsp each of chopped fresh coriander (cilantro) and mint into about 250ml/8fl oz/1 cup set yogurt. Season with salt, ground toasted cumin seeds and a pinch of sugar.
• For a cucumber dip, stir half a diced cucumber and 1 seeded and chopped fresh green chilli into 250ml/8fl oz/1 cup set yogurt. Season with salt and cumin.

3 Add the chickpea flour and baking powder, then use your hand to mix all the ingredients thoroughly.

4 Shape the mixture by hand into 12–15 koftas about the size of golf balls.

5 Heat the oil for deep-frying to 180–190°C/350–375°F or until a cube of day-old bread browns in about 30–45 seconds. Fry the koftas, four or five at a time, until deep golden brown all over. Drain on kitchen paper and keep warm until all the koftas are cooked. Serve with lemon wedges, coriander sprigs and a yogurt dip.

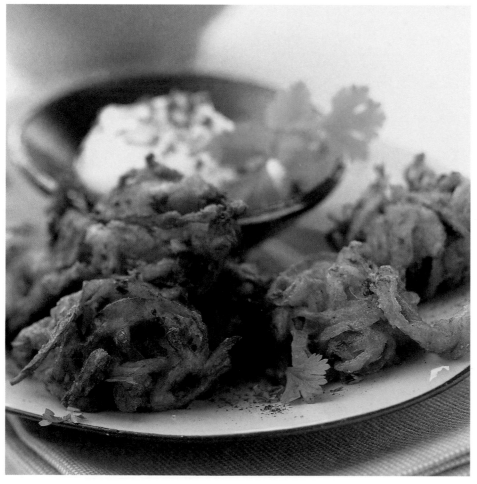

GRILLED POLENTA <u>WITH</u> CARAMELIZED ONIONS, RADICCHIO <u>AND</u> TALEGGIO CHEESE

SLICES OF GRILLED POLENTA, ONE OF THE STAPLES OF NORTH ITALIAN COOKING, ARE TASTY TOPPED WITH SLOWLY CARAMELIZED ONIONS AND BUBBLING TALEGGIO CHEESE, ALSO FROM NORTH ITALY.

<u>SERVES FOUR</u>

INGREDIENTS
  900ml/1½ pints/3¾ cups water
  5ml/1 tsp salt
  150g/5oz/generous 1 cup polenta
    or corn meal
  50g/2oz/⅔ cup freshly grated
    Parmesan cheese
  5ml/1 tsp chopped fresh thyme
  90ml/6 tbsp olive oil
  675g/1½lb onions, halved and sliced
  2 garlic cloves, chopped
  a few fresh thyme sprigs
  5ml/1 tsp brown sugar
  15–30ml/1–2 tbsp balsamic vinegar
  2 heads radicchio, cut into thick
    slices or wedges
  225g/8oz Taleggio cheese, sliced
  salt and ground black pepper

1 In a large pan, bring the water to the boil and add the salt. Adjust the heat so that it simmers. Stirring constantly, add the polenta in a steady stream, then bring to the boil. Cook over a very low heat, stirring frequently, for 30–40 minutes, until thick and smooth.

2 Beat in the Parmesan and chopped thyme, then turn on to a work surface or tray. Spread evenly, then leave to cool.

3 Heat 30ml/2 tbsp of the oil in a frying pan over a moderate heat. Add the onions and stir to coat in the oil, then cover and cook over a very low heat for 15 minutes, stirring occasionally.

4 Add the garlic and most of the thyme sprigs and cook, uncovered, for another 10 minutes, or until light brown.

5 Add the sugar, 15ml/1 tbsp of the vinegar and salt and pepper. Cook for another 5–10 minutes, until soft and well-browned. Taste and add more vinegar and seasoning as necessary.

6 Preheat the grill (broiler). Cut the polenta into thick slices and brush with a little of the remaining oil, then grill (broil) until crusty and lightly browned.

7 Turn over the polenta and add the radicchio to the grill rack or pan. Season the radicchio and brush with a little oil. Grill for about 5 minutes, until the polenta and radicchio are browned. Drizzle a little vinegar over the radicchio.

8 Heap the onions on to the polenta. Sprinkle the cheese and a few sprigs of thyme over both polenta and radicchio. Grill until the cheese is bubbling. Season with pepper and serve immediately.

ONION TART

NO BOOK ON ONION COOKING WOULD BE COMPLETE WITHOUT A RECIPE FOR THIS CLASSIC TART FROM ALSACE IN EASTERN FRANCE. TRADITIONALLY SERVED IN SMALL SLICES AS A FIRST COURSE, IT ALSO MAKES A DELICIOUS MAIN COURSE WHEN SERVED WARM AND ACCOMPANIED BY A GREEN SALAD.

SERVES FOUR TO SIX

INGREDIENTS
175g/6oz/1½ cups plain (all-
    purpose) flour
75g/3oz/6 tbsp butter, chilled
30–45ml/2–3 tbsp iced water
For the filling
50g/2oz/¼ cup butter
900g/2lb Spanish (Bermuda) onions,
    thinly sliced
1 egg plus 2 egg yolks
250ml/8fl oz/1 cup double
    (heavy) cream
1.5ml/¼ tsp freshly grated nutmeg
salt and ground black pepper

VARIATIONS
There are endless variations on this tart: try adding chopped fresh herbs such as thyme. The tart is also delicious made with cheese pastry; add 50g/2oz/⅔ cup grated Parmesan to the flour.

1 Process the flour, a pinch of salt and the chilled butter in a food processor until reduced to fine crumbs. Add the iced water and process briefly to form a dough. Wrap in clear film (plastic wrap) and chill for 40 minutes.

2 Melt the butter in a large pan and add the onions and a pinch of salt. Turn them in the butter. Cover and cook very gently, stirring frequently, for 30–40 minutes. Cool slightly.

3 Preheat the oven to 190°C/375°F/ Gas 5. Roll out the dough thinly and use to line a 23–25cm/9–10in loose-based flan tin (tart pan). Line with foil or baking parchment and baking beans, then bake blind for 10 minutes.

4 Remove the foil or parchment and baking beans, and bake for another 4–5 minutes, until the pastry is lightly cooked to a pale brown colour (blonde is a good description). Reduce the oven temperature to 180°C/350°F/Gas 4.

5 Beat the egg, egg yolks and cream together. Season with salt, pepper and the grated nutmeg. Place half the onions in the pastry case (pie shell) and add half the egg mixture. Add the remaining onions, then pour in as much of the remaining custard as you can.

6 Place on a baking sheet and bake on the middle shelf for 40–50 minutes, or until the custard is risen, browned and set in the centre. Serve warm rather than piping hot.

BEAN SALAD WITH TUNA AND RED ONION

THIS MAKES A GREAT FIRST COURSE OR EVEN A LIGHT MAIN MEAL IF SERVED WITH A GREEN SALAD, SOME GARLIC MAYONNAISE AND PLENTY OF WARM, CRUSTY BREAD.

SERVES FOUR

INGREDIENTS
    250g/9oz/1⅓ cups dried haricot
        (navy) or cannellini beans, soaked
        overnight in cold water
    1 bay leaf
    200–250g/7–9oz fine green
        beans, trimmed
    1 large red onion, very thinly sliced
    45ml/3 tbsp chopped fresh flat
        leaf parsley
    200–250g/7–9oz good-quality
        canned tuna in olive oil, drained
    200g/7oz cherry tomatoes, halved
    salt and ground black pepper
    a few onion rings, to garnish
For the dressing
    90ml/6 tbsp extra virgin olive oil
    15ml/1 tbsp tarragon vinegar
    5ml/1 tsp tarragon mustard
    1 garlic clove, finely chopped
    5ml/1 tsp grated lemon rind
    a little lemon juice
    pinch of caster (superfine) sugar

1 Drain the beans and bring them to the boil in fresh water with the bay leaf added. Boil rapidly for 10 minutes, then reduce the heat and boil steadily for 1–1½ hours, until tender. The cooking time depends on the age of the beans. Drain well. Discard the bay leaf.

2 Meanwhile, place all the dressing ingredients apart from the lemon juice and sugar in a jug (pitcher) or bowl and whisk until mixed. Season to taste with salt, pepper, lemon juice and a pinch of sugar. Leave to stand.

3 Blanch the green beans in plenty of boiling water for 3–4 minutes. Drain, refresh under cold water and drain thoroughly again.

4 Place both types of beans in a bowl. Add half the dressing and toss to mix. Stir in the onion and half the chopped parsley, then season to taste with salt and pepper.

5 Flake the tuna into large chunks with a knife and toss it into the beans with the tomato halves.

6 Arrange the salad on four individual plates. Drizzle the remaining dressing over the salad and sprinkle the remaining chopped parsley on top. Garnish with a few onion rings and serve immediately, at room temperature.

Baked Stuffed Onions
<u>with</u> Tomato Sauce

These are ideal comfort food for supper on cold winter evenings. Serve with buttered
cabbage and rice or thick slices of bread to mop up the sauce.

<u>SERVES EIGHT</u>

INGREDIENTS
   8 onions, each about 8.5cm/3½in
      in diameter, peeled but left whole
   60ml/4 tbsp olive oil
   2.5ml/½ tsp ground allspice
   50g/2oz pancetta or bacon, chopped
   250g/9oz minced (ground) pork
   115g/4oz/2 cups fresh breadcrumbs
   45ml/3 tbsp chopped fresh parsley
   15ml/1 tbsp chopped fresh oregano
   1.5ml/½ tsp ground cinnamon
   75ml/5 tbsp water
   25g/1oz/2 tbsp butter
For the tomato sauce
   30ml/2 tbsp olive oil
   1 garlic clove, finely chopped
   2.5ml/½ tsp ground allspice
   400g/14oz can chopped tomatoes
   small piece of cinnamon stick
   1 fresh bay leaf
   30ml/2 tbsp chopped fresh oregano
   30ml/2 tbsp double (heavy) cream
   1.5–2.5ml/¼–½ tsp harissa or other
      chilli paste
   pinch of brown sugar (optional)
   salt and ground black pepper

1 Place the onions in a large pan, pour in water to cover and bring to the boil. Reduce the heat and simmer gently for 10–15 minutes. Drain and cool.

2 Cut a small cap off the top of each onion. Use a small, sharp knife and a teaspoon to hollow out the centres, leaving a shell of two or three layers.

3 Stand the onion shells in a large ovenproof dish and patch any holes in their bases with pieces of onion. Chop the flesh removed from the centres and set aside 45ml/3 tbsp for the sauce. Heat 30ml/2 tbsp of the oil in a frying pan and cook the chopped onion over a low heat until just beginning to brown. Add the allspice and cook for a little longer. Remove and set aside.

4 Cook the pancetta or bacon in the pan until the fat melts. Add the pork and cook until it is beginning to brown. Preheat the oven to 190°C/375°F/Gas 5.

5 Place 75g/3oz/1½ cups of the breadcrumbs in a bowl and add the cooked onions, pork, half the parsley, the oregano and the ground cinnamon. Season well and mix to form a stuffing.

6 Fill the onions with the stuffing. Spoon the water around the onions and dot the butter on top of them. Cover with foil and bake for 30 minutes.

7 To make the sauce, heat the oil and cook the reserved onion and the garlic until soft and just beginning to brown. Add the allspice and cook for about 2 minutes, then add the tomatoes, cinnamon stick, bay leaf and oregano. Cook, uncovered, for 15–20 minutes.

8 Remove the cinnamon and bay leaf. Process the sauce in a blender or food processor until smooth. Add 45–60ml/ 3–4 tbsp water to thin to a pouring consistency. Add the cream with seasoning, harissa and sugar to taste.

9 Pour the sauce around the onions and use it to baste them. Cover the dish and bake for 20–25 minutes, then uncover and baste again. Mix together the remaining breadcrumbs and parsley. Sprinkle the crumbs over the onions, then drizzle with the remaining 30ml/2 tbsp of oil. Return the dish to the oven and bake for 15–20 minutes, until the topping is browned and crisp. Serve immediately.

JANSSON'S TEMPTATION

A traditional Swedish favourite, this rich gratin is thought to be named after Adolf Janzon, a star of the Royal Opera House, Stockholm. Janzon would invite his friends to dinner after a performance, serving them this delicious potato dish.

SERVES FOUR TO SIX

INGREDIENTS

50g/2oz/¼ cup butter
900g/2lb waxy potatoes
2 large sweet Spanish (Bermuda)
  onions, sliced
2 × 50g/2oz cans anchovies in olive
  oil, drained
450ml/¾ pint/scant 2 cups whipping
  cream or half and half double
  (heavy) and single (light) cream
a little milk (optional)
salt and ground black pepper

1 Preheat the oven to 200°C/400°F/ Gas 6. Use 15g/½oz/1 tbsp of the butter to grease a 1.5 litre/2½ pint/6¼ cup ovenproof dish.

2 Using a sharp knife, carefully cut the potatoes into fine batons.

3 Toss the potato batons with salt and freshly ground black pepper and sprinkle half of them in the base of the prepared ovenproof dish.

4 Lay half of the onions on top of the potatoes, season with black pepper and dot with butter. Lay the anchovies on top of the onions, then add the rest of the sliced onions and top with the remaining potatoes.

5 Mix the cream with 30ml/2 tbsp cold water and pour this over the potatoes. Add a little milk, if necessary, to bring the liquid to just below the top of the final layer of potatoes.

6 Dot the potatoes with the remaining butter then cover with foil and bake for 1 hour.

7 Reduce the heat to 180°C/350°F/ Gas 4 and uncover the dish. Bake for a further 40–50 minutes or until the potatoes are tender and brown.

COOK'S TIPS
• Cover the gratin with foil for the first half of cooking so that the potatoes don't brown or dry out too much. If using whole, salted anchovies or Swedish salted sprats they will need to be boned. If they are very salty, soak in a little milk for 30 minutes before using.
• Serve with small glasses of chilled schnapps and cold beer for an authentic Swedish flavour.

PASTA <u>WITH</u> SLOWLY COOKED ONIONS, CABBAGE, PARMESAN <u>AND</u> PINE NUTS

THIS IS AN UNUSUAL, BUT QUITE DELICIOUS, WAY OF SERVING PASTA. CAVOLO NERO, TUSCAN BLACK CABBAGE, IS A CLOSE RELATIVE OF CURLY KALE, WITH LONG LEAVES AND A SPICY FLAVOUR.

SERVES FOUR

INGREDIENTS
25g/1oz/2 tbsp butter
15ml/1 tbsp extra virgin olive oil,
  plus extra for drizzling (optional)
500g/1¼lb Spanish (Bermuda)
  onions, halved and thinly sliced
5–10ml/1–2 tsp balsamic vinegar
400–500g/14oz–20oz cavolo nero,
  spring greens (collards), kale or
  Brussels sprout tops, shredded
400–500g/14–20oz dried pasta (such
  as penne or fusilli)
75g/3oz/1 cup freshly grated
  Parmesan cheese
50g/2oz/½ cup pine nuts, toasted
salt and ground black pepper

VARIATION
To make a delicious pilaff, cook 250g/
9oz/1¼ cups brown basmati rice and use
in place of the pasta.

1 Heat the butter and olive oil together in a large, heavy pan. Stir in the onions, cover and cook very gently, stirring occasionally, for about 20 minutes, until very soft.

2 Uncover, and continue to cook gently, until the onions have turned golden yellow. Add the balsamic vinegar and season well, then cook for a further 1–2 minutes. Set aside.

3 Blanch the cavolo nero, spring greens, kale or Brussels sprout tops in lightly salted, boiling water for about 3 minutes. Drain well and add to the onions, then cook over a low heat for 3–4 minutes.

4 Cook the pasta in lightly salted, boiling water for 8–12 minutes, or according to the packet instructions, until just tender. Drain, then add to the pan of onions and greens and toss thoroughly to mix.

5 Season well with salt and pepper and stir in half the Parmesan. Transfer the pasta to warmed plates. Sprinkle the pine nuts and more Parmesan on top and serve immediately, offering extra olive oil for drizzling over to taste.

LAMB SMOTHERED IN ONIONS AND NORTH AFRICAN SPICES

THIS IS A WONDERFUL WAY OF COOKING A LEG OR SHOULDER OF LAMB, BY FIRST MARINATING IT IN YOGURT WITH NORTH AFRICAN SPICES, THEN COVERING WITH SLICED ONIONS AND POT-ROASTING. SERVE A COUSCOUS PILAFF AND YOGURT FLAVOURED WITH GARLIC AS ACCOMPANIMENTS.

SERVES SIX

INGREDIENTS

  2kg/4½lb leg or shoulder of lamb
  30ml/2 tbsp olive oil
  2 large onions, halved and sliced
  3 fresh bay leaves
  300ml/½ pint/1¼ cups water
  500g/1¼lb butternut squash, peeled,
    seeded and cut into thick chunks
  2–3 green or red (bell) peppers,
    seeded and cut into thick slices
  chopped fresh coriander (cilantro)
For the spice paste
  15ml/1 tbsp cumin seeds
  15ml/1 tbsp coriander seeds
  2.5cm/1in piece cinnamon stick
  7.5ml/1½ tsp paprika
  good pinch of saffron threads
  1 green chilli, seeded and chopped
  2 garlic cloves, chopped
  15g/½oz fresh coriander
    (cilantro), chopped
  30ml/2 tbsp fresh mint, chopped
  45ml/3 tbsp extra virgin olive oil
  grated rind and juice of 1 lemon
  250ml/8fl oz/1 cup plain
    (natural) yogurt
  salt and ground black pepper

1 First prepare the spice paste. Set 5ml/1 tsp each of the cumin and coriander seeds aside and toast the remainder separately in a small dry pan until they are aromatic. Take care not to overcook the spices or cook them too quickly or they will taste bitter.

2 Grind the toasted spices with the cinnamon in a spice or coffee grinder. Then process them with all the paste ingredients, apart from the yogurt, in a food processor or blender to make a paste. Season with salt and pepper.

3 Use a sharp knife to make deep slits all over the lamb, then rub the spice paste all over, forcing it into the slits. Place the lamb in a roasting pan and rub the yogurt all over. Cover and marinate for several hours, preferably overnight, turning once or twice.

4 Preheat the oven to 180°C/350°F/ Gas 4. Scrape the marinade off the meat and reserve. Heat a large roasting pan in the oven and brown the lamb all over. Remove it and set aside. Add the oil and cook the onions for 6–8 minutes, until softened. Coarsely grind the reserved coriander and cumin seeds, add to the onions and cook for 2–3 minutes. Transfer the onions to a plate.

5 Add the marinade to the pan with the bay leaves and water. Bring to the boil. Return the lamb to the pan and turn it in the liquid. Cover with the onions, then cover the pan tightly with foil and cook in the oven for 1¾–2 hours, until tender. Baste the lamb occasionally and add a little more water if the dish seems dry. Remove the lamb and onions, cover and keep warm. Increase the oven temperature to 200°C/400°F/Gas 6.

6 Add the squash and peppers to the pan and toss in the lamb juices. Roast, uncovered, for 30–35 minutes, stirring once or twice, until the squash is tender. Return the lamb for the last 15 minutes.

7 Transfer the lamb and vegetables to a warmed serving dish and sprinkle with the fresh coriander. Serve immediately, cut into thick slices.

The delicate flavour of leeks adds subtle undertones and the gentlest hint of that special allium quality to dishes as diverse as soups, salads, gratins and pies. One of the most versatile members of the onion family, the unassuming leek complements and enhances a wide range of other ingredients, from chicken to fish and from mushrooms to cheese — characteristics superbly demonstrated in this delicious collection of international recipes.

Cooking with Leeks

CHICKEN AND LEEK SOUP WITH PRUNES AND BARLEY

THIS RECIPE IS BASED ON THE TRADITIONAL SCOTTISH SOUP, COCK-A-LEEKIE. THE UNUSUAL COMBINATION OF LEEKS AND PRUNES IS SURPRISINGLY DELICIOUS.

SERVES SIX

INGREDIENTS
    1 chicken, weighing about 2kg/4¼lb
    900g/2lb leeks
    1 fresh bay leaf
    a few each fresh parsley stalks and
       thyme sprigs
    1 large carrot, thickly sliced
    2.4 litres/4 pints/10 cups chicken or
       beef stock
    115g/4oz/generous ½ cup
       pearl barley
    400g/14oz ready-to-eat prunes
    salt and ground black pepper
    chopped fresh parsley, to garnish

1 Cut off the chicken breast portions and set aside. Place the remaining chicken carcass in a large pan. Cut half the leeks into 5cm/2in lengths and add them to the pan. Tie the bay leaf, parsley and thyme into a bouquet garni and add to the pan with the carrot and the stock. Bring to the boil, then reduce the heat and cover. Simmer gently for 1 hour. Skim off any scum when the water first boils and occasionally during simmering.

2 Add the breast portions and cook for another 30 minutes, until they are just cooked. Leave until cool enough to handle, then strain the stock. Reserve the breast portions and meat from the chicken carcass. Discard all the skin, bones, cooked vegetables and herbs. Skim as much fat as you can from the stock, then return it to the pan.

3 Meanwhile, rinse the pearl barley thoroughly in a sieve under cold running water, then cook it in a large pan of boiling water for about 10 minutes. Drain, rinse well again and drain thoroughly.

4 Add the pearl barley to the stock. Bring to the boil over a medium heat, then lower the heat and cook very gently for 15–20 minutes, until the barley is just cooked and tender. Season the soup with 5ml/1 tsp salt and black pepper.

5 Add the prunes. Slice the remaining leeks and add them to the pan. Bring to the boil, then simmer for 10 minutes or until the leeks are just cooked.

6 Slice the chicken breast portions and add them to the soup with the remaining chicken meat, sliced or cut into neat pieces. Reheat if necessary, then ladle the soup into deep plates and sprinkle with chopped parsley.

MEDITERRANEAN LEEK AND FISH SOUP WITH TOMATOES

THIS CHUNKY SOUP, WHICH IS ALMOST A STEW, MAKES A ROBUST AND WONDERFULLY AROMATIC MEAL IN A BOWL. SERVE IT WITH CRISP-BAKED CROÛTES SPREAD WITH A SPICY GARLIC MAYONNAISE.

SERVES FOUR

INGREDIENTS

  30ml/2 tbsp olive oil
  2 large thick leeks, white and green
    parts separated, both thinly sliced
  5ml/1 tsp crushed coriander seeds
  good pinch of dried red chilli flakes
  300g/11oz small salad potatoes,
    thickly sliced
  200g/7oz can chopped tomatoes
  600ml/1 pint/2½ cups fish stock
  150ml/¼ pint/⅔ cup fruity white wine
  1 fresh bay leaf
  1 star anise
  strip of pared orange rind
  good pinch of saffron threads
  450g/1lb white fish fillets, such as
    monkfish, sea bass, cod or haddock
  450g/1lb small squid, cleaned
  250g/9oz uncooked peeled
    prawns (shrimp)
  30–45ml/2–3 tbsp chopped parsley
  salt and ground black pepper
To serve
  1 short French loaf, sliced and toasted
  spicy garlic mayonnaise

1 Gently heat the oil in a pan, then add the green part of the leeks, the coriander and the chilli, and cook for 5 minutes.

2 Add the potatoes and tomatoes and pour in the stock and wine. Add the bay leaf, star anise, orange rind and saffron.

3 Bring to the boil, reduce the heat and part-cover the pan. Simmer for 20 minutes or until the potatoes are tender. Taste and adjust the seasoning.

4 Cut the fish into chunks. Cut the squid sacs into rectangles and score a criss-cross pattern into them without cutting right through.

5 Add the fish to the stew and cook gently for 4 minutes. Add the prawns and cook for 1 minute. Add the squid and the shredded white part of the leek and cook, stirring occasionally, for 2 minutes.

6 Stir in the chopped parsley and serve with toasted French bread and spicy garlic mayonnaise.

GRILLED LEEK AND FENNEL SALAD WITH SPICY TOMATO DRESSING

THIS IS AN EXCELLENT SALAD TO MAKE IN THE EARLY AUTUMN WHEN YOUNG LEEKS ARE AT THEIR BEST AND RIPE TOMATOES ARE FULL OF FLAVOUR. SERVE WITH GOOD BREAD AS AN APPETIZER OR SERVE TO ACCOMPANY SIMPLY GRILLED WHITE FISH FOR A MAIN COURSE.

SERVES SIX AS AN APPETIZER

INGREDIENTS
675g/1½lb leeks
2 large fennel bulbs
120ml/4fl oz/½ cup extra virgin olive oil
2 shallots, chopped
150ml/¼ pint/⅔ cup dry white wine or white vermouth
5ml/1 tsp fennel seeds, crushed
6 fresh thyme sprigs
2–3 bay leaves
good pinch of dried red chilli flakes
350g/12oz tomatoes, peeled, seeded and diced
5ml/1 tsp sun-dried tomato paste
good pinch of caster (superfine) sugar (optional)
75g/3oz/¾ cup small black olives
salt and ground black pepper

2 Trim the fennel bulbs, reserving any feathery tops for the garnish and cut the bulbs either into thin slices or into thicker wedges, according to taste.

3 Cook the fennel in the reserved cooking water for about 5 minutes, then drain thoroughly and toss with 30ml/ 2 tbsp of the olive oil. Season to taste with black pepper.

6 Add the diced tomatoes and cook briskly for 5–8 minutes, or until reduced and thickened.

7 Add the tomato paste and adjust the seasoning to taste, adding a good pinch of caster sugar if you think the dressing needs it.

1 Cook the leeks in salted, boiling water for 4–5 minutes. Use a slotted spoon to remove the leeks and place them in a colander to drain thoroughly and cool. Reserve the cooking water in the pan. Squeeze out excess water and cut the leeks into 7.5cm/3in lengths.

COOK'S TIP
When buying fennel, look for rounded bulbs; they have a better shape for this dish. The flesh should be crisp and white, with no signs of bruising. Avoid specimens with broken leaves or with brown or dried out patches.

4 Heat a ridged cast-iron griddle. Arrange the leeks and fennel on the griddle and cook until tinged deep brown, turning once. Remove the vegetables from the griddle, place in a large shallow dish and set aside.

5 Place the remaining olive oil, the shallots, white wine or vermouth, crushed fennel seeds, thyme, bay leaves and chilli flakes in a large pan and bring to the boil over a medium heat. Lower the heat and simmer for 10 minutes.

8 Pour the dressing over the leeks and fennel, toss to mix and leave to cool. The salad may be made several hours in advance and kept in the refrigerator, but bring it back to room temperature before serving.

9 When ready to serve, stir the salad then sprinkle the chopped fennel tops and black olives over the top.

LEEK, SQUASH AND TOMATO GRATIN

THIS AUTUMNAL GRATIN COMPLEMENTS ROAST OR GRILLED LAMB OR CHICKEN. OR SERVE IT AS A SIMPLE SUPPER DISH ACCOMPANIED BY A GREEN SALAD AND GOOD BREAD.

4 Heat the cream in a small pan with the chilli and garlic. Bring to the boil, then stir in the mint and pour over the gratin, thoroughly scraping the contents out of the pan.

SERVES FOUR TO SIX

INGREDIENTS
  450g/1lb peeled and seeded squash,
    cut into 1cm/½in slices
  60ml/4 tbsp olive oil
  450g/1lb leeks, cut into thick,
    diagonal slices
  675g/1½lb tomatoes, peeled and
    thickly sliced
  2.5ml/½ tsp ground toasted cumin seeds
  450ml/¾ pint/scant 2 cups single
    (light) cream
  1 fresh red chilli, seeded and sliced
  1 garlic clove, finely chopped
  15ml/1 tbsp chopped fresh mint
  30ml/2 tbsp chopped fresh parsley
  60ml/4 tbsp fine white breadcrumbs
  salt and ground black pepper

1 Steam the squash over boiling salted water for 10 minutes.

2 Heat half the oil in a frying pan and cook the leeks gently for 5–6 minutes, until lightly coloured. Try to keep the slices intact. Preheat the oven to 190°C/375°F/Gas 5.

3 Layer the squash, leeks and tomatoes in a 2 litre/3½ pint/8¾ cup gratin dish, arranging them in rows. Season with salt, pepper and cumin.

5 Bake for 50–55 minutes, or until the gratin is bubbling and the vegetables are tender. Sprinkle the parsley and breadcrumbs on top and drizzle over the remaining oil. Then bake for another 15–20 minutes until the breadcrumbs are browned and crisp. Serve immediately.

BRAISED LEEKS WITH CARROTS

SWEET CARROTS AND LEEKS GO WELL TOGETHER AND ARE GOOD FINISHED WITH A LITTLE CHOPPED MINT, CHERVIL OR PARSLEY. THIS IS A GOOD ACCOMPANIMENT TO ROAST BEEF, LAMB OR CHICKEN.

SERVES SIX

INGREDIENTS
- 65g/2½oz/5 tbsp butter
- 675g/1½lb carrots, thickly sliced
- 2 fresh bay leaves
- pinch of caster (superfine) sugar
- 75ml/5 tbsp water
- 675g/1½lb leeks, cut into 5cm/ 2in lengths
- 120ml/4fl oz/½ cup white wine
- 30ml/2 tbsp chopped fresh mint, chervil or parsley
- salt and ground black pepper

1 Melt 25g/1oz/2 tbsp of the butter in a pan and cook the carrots gently, without allowing them to brown, for 4–5 minutes.

2 Add the bay leaves, seasoning, the sugar and water. Bring to the boil, cover and cook for 10–15 minutes, until the carrots are tender. Uncover, then boil until the juices have evaporated, leaving the carrots moist and glazed.

3 Meanwhile, melt another 25g/1oz/ 2 tbsp of the remaining butter in a wide pan or deep frying pan that will take the leeks in a single layer. Add the leeks and cook them in the butter over a low heat for 4–5 minutes, without allowing them to brown.

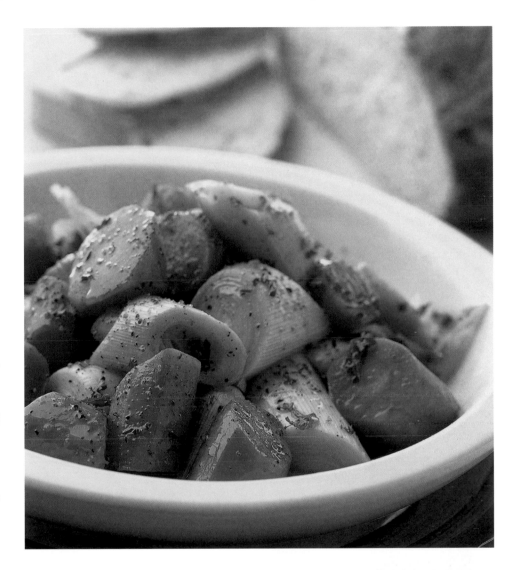

5 Uncover the leeks and turn them in the buttery juices. Increase the heat, then boil the liquid rapidly until reduced to a few tablespoons.

VARIATION
Braised leeks in tarragon cream
Cook 900g/2lb leeks in 40g/1½oz/3 tbsp butter as above. Season, add a pinch of sugar, 45ml/3 tbsp tarragon vinegar, 6 fresh tarragon sprigs or 5ml/1 tsp dried tarragon and 60ml/4 tbsp white wine. Cover and cook as above. Add 150ml/ ¼ pint/⅔ cup double (heavy) cream and allow to bubble. Adjust the seasoning and serve sprinkled with chopped fresh tarragon. A spoonful of tarragon-flavoured mustard is good stirred into these leeks.

4 Add seasoning, a good pinch of sugar, the wine and half the chopped herb. Heat until simmering, then cover and cook gently for 5–8 minutes, until the leeks are tender, but not collapsed.

6 Add the carrots to the leeks and reheat them gently, then swirl in the remaining butter. Adjust the seasoning, if necessary. Transfer to a warmed serving dish and serve sprinkled with the remaining chopped herb.

LEEKS BAKED WITH HAM, CREAM AND MINT

CHOOSE LEEKS THAT ARE NOT TOO THICK FOR THIS VERY EASY BUT DELICIOUS SUPPER DISH.
SERVE GOOD BREAD TO MOP UP THE SAUCE AND A GREEN SALAD TO REFRESH THE PALATE.

SERVES FOUR

INGREDIENTS
8–12 slender leeks
8–12 large, medium-thick slices
   prosciutto or Serrano ham
15g/½oz/1 tbsp butter
75g/3oz/1 cup freshly grated
   Parmesan cheese
250ml/8fl oz/1 cup double
   (heavy) cream
15ml/1 tbsp chopped fresh mint
pinch of cayenne pepper
45ml/3 tbsp fine white breadcrumbs
salt and ground black pepper

1 Trim the leeks so that they are all the same size. Bring a large pan of lightly salted water to the boil, add the leeks and cook for 5–8 minutes. Test the leeks with the tip of a sharp knife to check if they are cooked. Drain, reserving 60ml/4 tbsp of the cooking water. Squeeze the excess water out of the leeks. Preheat the oven to 190°C/375°F/Gas 5.

VARIATIONS
• Arrange the leeks on a bed of 350g/12oz ripe tomatoes, peeled, seeded and finely chopped.
• Wrap the cooked leeks in fried, but not crisp, bacon. Then pour over a cheese sauce made with equal quantities of the reserved cooking water and milk. Season the sauce to taste with Dijon mustard, grated Cheddar cheese and nutmeg. Sprinkle with grated Parmesan and fine white breadcrumbs and bake as above.
• Wrap 8 raw, slender leeks in slices of pancetta or prosciutto, then fry gently in 25g/1oz/2 tbsp butter for 5 minutes. Add 90ml/6 tbsp white wine and some sprigs of thyme and season to taste with salt and pepper. Cover and cook very gently for 15–20 minutes, until the leeks are cooked. Remove the leeks from the pan, increase the heat and add 60ml/4 tbsp double (heavy) cream, then bubble to make a sauce. Adjust the seasoning and pour over the leeks. Sprinkle with a little chopped parsley before serving.

2 Wrap each leek in a slice of ham. Butter an ovenproof gratin dish just large enough to take the leeks in one layer and arrange the leeks in it. Season to taste with salt and pepper and sprinkle half the grated Parmesan cheese over the leeks.

3 Mix the cream, cooking water and mint. Season with salt, pepper and cayenne and pour over the leeks. Sprinkle the breadcrumbs and the remaining Parmesan on top. Bake for 30–35 minutes, until bubbling and browned. Serve immediately.

SALMON EN PAPILLOTE <u>WITH</u> LEEKS <u>AND</u> YELLOW PEPPERS

COOKING FISH "EN PAPILLOTE" MAKES A LOT OF SENSE, MAKING SURE THAT THE FISH RETAINS ITS FLAVOUR WHILE IT COOKS IN ITS PARCEL WITH AROMATIC INGREDIENTS SUCH AS LEEKS AND HERBS. IT IS ALSO EXCELLENT WHEN ENTERTAINING, AS THE PARCELS MAY BE PREPARED AHEAD OF COOKING.

SERVES SIX

INGREDIENTS
   25ml/1½ tbsp groundnut (peanut) oil
   2 yellow (bell) peppers, seeded and
      thinly sliced
   4cm/1½in fresh root ginger, peeled
      and finely shredded
   1 large fennel bulb, thinly sliced,
      feathery tops chopped and reserved
   1 green chilli, seeded and
      finely shredded
   2 large leeks, cut into 10cm/4in
      lengths and shredded lengthways
   30ml/2 tbsp chopped chives
   10ml/2 tsp light soy sauce
   6 portions salmon fillet, each
      weighing 150–175g/5–6oz, skinned
   10ml/2 tsp toasted sesame oil
   salt and ground black pepper

1 Heat the oil in a large non-stick frying pan and cook the peppers, ginger and fennel for 5–6 minutes, until they are softened but not browned. Add the chilli and leeks and cook for a further 2–3 minutes. Stir in half the chives and the soy sauce with seasoning to taste. Set aside to cool.

2 Preheat the oven to 190°C/375°F/Gas 5. Cut 6 × 35cm/14in rounds of baking parchment or foil. Divide the vegetable mixture between the 6 rounds and place a portion of salmon on each pile of vegetables. Drizzle with sesame oil and sprinkle with the remaining chives and the chopped fennel tops. Season with salt and pepper.

3 Fold the paper or foil over to enclose the fish, rolling and twisting the edges together to seal the parcels. Place the parcels on a baking sheet and bake for 15–20 minutes, until the parcels are puffed up and, if made with paper, lightly browned. Transfer the parcels to warmed individual plates and serve immediately.

POTATO AND LEEK FILO PIE

THIS FILO PASTRY PIE MAKES AN ATTRACTIVE AND UNUSUAL CENTREPIECE FOR A VEGETARIAN BUFFET.
SERVE IT COOL, WITH A CHOICE OF SALADS.

SERVES EIGHT

INGREDIENTS
  800g/1¾lb new potatoes, sliced
  400g/14oz leeks (trimmed weight)
  75g/3oz/6 tbsp butter
  15g/½oz parsley, finely chopped
  60ml/4 tbsp chopped mixed fresh
    herbs (such as chervil, chives, a
    little tarragon and basil)
  12 sheets filo pastry
  150g/5oz white Cheshire,
    Lancashire or Cantal
    cheese, sliced
  2 garlic cloves, finely chopped
  250ml/8fl oz/1 cup double
    (heavy) cream
  2 large (US extra large) egg yolks
  salt and ground black pepper

1 Preheat the oven to 190°C/375°F/
Gas 5. Cook the potatoes in lightly
salted, boiling water for 3–4 minutes,
then drain and set aside.

2 Slice the leeks. Melt 25g/1oz/2 tbsp
of the butter in a frying pan and cook
the leeks gently, stirring occasionally,
until softened. Remove from the heat,
season with pepper and stir in half the
parsley and half the mixed herbs.

3 Melt the remaining butter. Line a
23cm/9in loose-based metal cake tin
(pan) with six or seven sheets of filo
pastry, brushing each layer with butter.
Let the edges overhang the rim.

4 Layer the potatoes, leeks and cheese
in the tin, sprinkling a few herbs and
the garlic between the layers. Season.

5 Flip the overhanging pastry over the
filling and cover with two sheets of filo,
tucking in the sides to fit and brushing
with melted butter as before. Cover
the pie loosely with foil and bake for
35 minutes. (Keep the remaining pastry
covered with a plastic bag and a clean,
damp cloth.)

6 Meanwhile beat the cream, egg yolks
and remaining herbs together. Make a
hole in the centre of the pie and
gradually pour in the eggs and cream.

7 Arrange the remaining pastry on top,
teasing it into swirls and folds, then
brush with melted butter. Reduce the
oven temperature to 180°C/350°F/
Gas 4 and bake the pie for another
25–30 minutes, until the top is golden
and crisp. Allow to cool before serving.

LEEK AND ROQUEFORT TART WITH WALNUT PASTRY

MILD LEEKS GO EXCEPTIONALLY WELL WITH THE SALTY FLAVOUR OF THE ROQUEFORT CHEESE, AND THE NUTTINESS OF THE PASTRY MARRIES THE INGREDIENTS PERFECTLY IN THIS TART. SERVE THE TART WARM WITH A PEPPERY GREEN SALAD OF ROCKET, MIZUNA OR WATERCRESS.

SERVES FOUR TO SIX

INGREDIENTS
    25g/1oz/2 tbsp butter
    450g/1lb leeks, sliced
    175g/6oz Roquefort cheese, sliced
    2 large (US extra large) eggs
    250ml/8fl oz/1 cup double
        (heavy) cream
    10ml/2 tsp chopped fresh tarragon
    salt and ground black pepper
For the pastry
    175g/6oz/1½ cups plain (all-
        purpose) flour
    50g/2oz/¼ cup butter
    75g/3oz/¾ cup walnuts, ground
    15ml/1 tbsp lemon juice
    30ml/2 tbsp iced water

1 First make the pastry. Sift the flour, 2.5ml/½ tsp salt and some black pepper into a bowl. Rub in the butter until the mixture looks like breadcrumbs, then stir in the ground walnuts. Bind with the lemon juice and iced water. Gather into a ball, wrap and chill for 30–40 minutes.

2 Preheat the oven to 190°C/375°F/ Gas 5. Roll out the pastry and use to line a 21–23cm/8½–9in loose-based metal flan tin (tart pan).

COOK'S TIP
Grind walnuts in a small food processor or clean coffee mill with a little of the pastry flour.

3 Protect the sides of the pastry with foil, prick the base with a fork and bake for 15 minutes. Remove the foil and bake for a further 5–10 minutes, until just firm to the touch. Reduce the oven temperature to 180°C/350°F/Gas 4.

4 Meanwhile, to make the filling, melt the butter in a pan, add the leeks, cover and cook for 10 minutes. Season and cook for a further 10 minutes. Cool.

5 Spoon the leeks into the pastry case and arrange the slices of Roquefort on top. Beat the eggs with the cream and season with pepper (the cheese will probably be sufficiently salty). Beat in the tarragon and carefully pour the mixture into the tart.

6 Bake the tart on the centre shelf of the oven for 30–40 minutes, until the filling has risen and browned and become firm to a gentle touch. Leave to cool for 10 minutes before serving.

BARLEY RISOTTO WITH ROASTED SQUASH AND LEEKS

THIS IS MORE LIKE A PILAFF, MADE WITH SLIGHTLY CHEWY, NUTTY-FLAVOURED PEARL BARLEY, THAN A CLASSIC RISOTTO. SWEET LEEKS AND ROASTED SQUASH ARE SUPERB WITH THIS EARTHY GRAIN.

3 Heat half the butter with the remaining oil in a large frying pan. Cook the leeks and garlic gently for 5 minutes. Add the mushrooms and remaining thyme, then cook until the liquid from the mushrooms evaporates and they begin to colour.

4 Stir in the carrots and cook for 2 minutes, then add the barley and most of the stock. Season well and part-cover the pan. Cook for a further 5 minutes. Pour in the remaining stock if the mixture seems dry.

5 Stir in the parsley, the remaining butter and half the Pecorino. Then stir in the squash. Add seasoning to taste and serve immediately, sprinkled with the toasted pumpkin seeds or walnuts and the remaining Pecorino.

SERVES FOUR TO FIVE

INGREDIENTS

  200g/7oz/1 cup pearl barley
  1 butternut squash, peeled, seeded and cut into chunks
  10ml/2 tsp chopped fresh thyme
  60ml/4 tbsp olive oil
  25g/1oz/2 tbsp butter
  4 leeks, cut into fairly thick diagonal slices
  2 garlic cloves, finely chopped
  175g/6oz chestnut mushrooms, sliced
  2 carrots, coarsely grated
  about 120ml/4fl oz/½ cup vegetable stock
  30ml/2 tbsp chopped fresh flat leaf parsley
  50g/2oz Pecorino cheese, grated or shaved
  45ml/3 tbsp pumpkin seeds, toasted, or chopped walnuts
  salt and ground black pepper

1 Rinse the barley, then cook it in simmering water, keeping the pan part-covered, for 35–45 minutes, or until tender. Drain. Preheat the oven to 200°C/400°F/Gas 6.

2 Place the squash in a roasting pan with half the thyme. Season with pepper and toss with half the oil. Roast, stirring once, for 30–35 minutes, until tender and beginning to brown.

Here is conclusive proof that garlic can be so much more than a mere accent, as it takes a starring role in soups, sauces, main course dishes and accompaniments. It complements fish and shellfish superbly, gives a much-needed lift to chicken, adds character to beef and turns routine vegetables into a taste sensation. And don't overlook tried and tested favourites, such as Garlic and Herb Bread, Aioli and Salsa Verde.

Dishes with Garlic

GARLIC AND CORIANDER SOUP

THIS RECIPE IS BASED ON THE WONDERFUL BREAD SOUPS OR AÇORDAS OF PORTUGAL. BEING A SIMPLE SOUP, IT SHOULD BE MADE WITH THE BEST INGREDIENTS — PLUMP GARLIC, FRESH CORIANDER, HIGH-QUALITY CRUSTY COUNTRY BREAD AND EXTRA VIRGIN OLIVE OIL.

SERVES SIX

INGREDIENTS
   25g/1oz/1 cup fresh coriander
     (cilantro), leaves and stalks
     chopped separately
   1.5 litres/2½ pints/6¼ cups vegetable
     or chicken stock
   5–6 plump garlic cloves, peeled
   6 eggs
   275g/10oz day-old bread, most of
     the crust removed and torn into
     bitesize pieces
   salt and ground black pepper
   90ml/6 tbsp extra virgin olive oil,
     plus extra to serve

1 Place the coriander stalks in a pan. Add the stock and bring to the boil, then simmer for 10 minutes. Process in a blender or food processor and sieve back into the pan.

2 Crush the garlic with 5ml/1 tsp salt, then stir in 120ml/4fl oz/½ cup hot soup. Return the mixture to the pan.

3 Meanwhile, poach the eggs in a frying pan of simmering water for about 3–4 minutes, until just set. Use a slotted spoon to remove them from the pan and transfer to a warmed plate. Trim off any untidy pieces of white.

4 Bring the soup back to the boil and add seasoning. Stir in the chopped coriander leaves and remove from the heat.

5 Place the bread in six soup plates or bowls and drizzle the oil over it. Ladle in the soup and stir. Add a poached egg to each bowl and serve immediately, offering olive oil at the table so that it can be drizzled over the soup to taste.

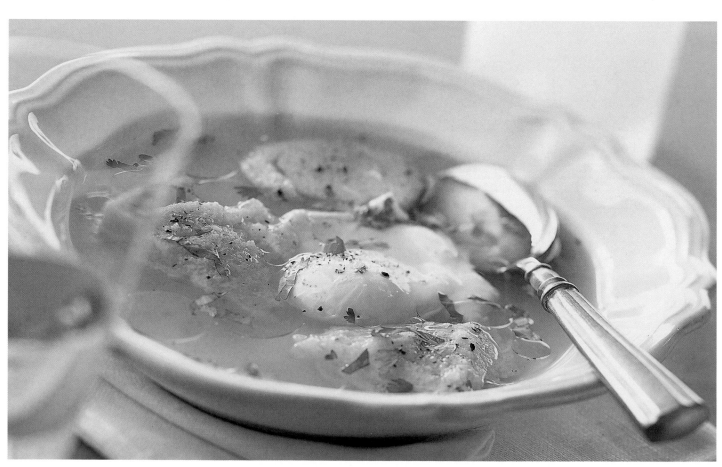

ROASTED GARLIC AND BUTTERNUT SQUASH SOUP WITH TOMATO SALSA

THIS IS A WONDERFUL, RICHLY FLAVOURED DISH. A SPOONFUL OF THE HOT AND SPICY TOMATO SALSA GIVES BITE TO THE SWEET-TASTING SQUASH AND GARLIC SOUP.

SERVES FOUR TO FIVE

INGREDIENTS
    2 garlic bulbs, outer papery
      skin removed
    75ml/5 tbsp olive oil
    a few fresh thyme sprigs
    1 large butternut squash, halved
      and seeded
    2 onions, chopped
    5ml/1 tsp ground coriander
    1.2 litres/2 pints/5 cups vegetable or
      chicken stock
    30–45ml/2–3 tbsp chopped fresh
      oregano or marjoram
    salt and ground black pepper
For the salsa
    4 large ripe tomatoes, halved
      and seeded
    1 red (bell) pepper, halved
      and seeded
    1 large fresh red chilli, halved
      and seeded
    30–45ml/2–3 tbsp olive oil
    15ml/1 tbsp balsamic vinegar
    pinch of caster (superfine) sugar

1 Preheat the oven to 220°C/425°F/ Gas 7. Place the garlic bulbs on a piece of foil and pour over half the olive oil. Add the thyme sprigs, then fold the foil around the garlic bulbs to enclose them completely. Place the foil parcel on a baking sheet with the butternut squash and brush the squash with 15ml/1 tbsp of the remaining olive oil. Add the tomatoes, red pepper and fresh chilli for the salsa.

2 Roast the vegetables for 25 minutes, then remove the tomatoes, pepper and chilli. Reduce the temperature to 190°C/375°F/Gas 5 and cook the squash and garlic for 20–25 minutes more, or until the squash is tender.

3 Heat the remaining oil in a large, heavy pan and cook the onions and ground coriander gently for about 10 minutes, or until softened.

4 Peel the pepper and chilli and process in a food processor or blender with the tomatoes and 30ml/2 tbsp olive oil. Stir in the vinegar and seasoning to taste, adding a pinch of caster sugar. Add the remaining oil if you think the salsa needs it.

5 Squeeze the roasted garlic out of its papery skin into the onions and scoop the squash out of its skin, adding it to the pan. Add the stock, 5ml/1 tsp salt and plenty of black pepper. Bring to the boil and simmer for 10 minutes.

6 Stir in half the oregano or marjoram and cool the soup slightly, then process it in a blender or food processor. Alternatively, press the soup through a fine sieve.

7 Reheat the soup without allowing it to boil, then taste for seasoning before ladling it into warmed bowls. Top each with a spoonful of salsa and sprinkle over the remaining chopped oregano or marjoram. Serve immediately.

MUSSELS ᴵᴺ GARLIC BUTTER

GARLIC AND HERB BUTTER IS A CLASSIC TREATMENT FOR SNAILS IN BURGUNDY, BUT BECAME VERY POPULAR IN THE 1960S WITH MUSSELS, AND MAKES A DELICIOUS FIRST COURSE.

SERVES FOUR

INGREDIENTS
  2kg/4½lb mussels, scrubbed
  2 large shallots, finely chopped
  200ml/7fl oz/scant 1 cup dry
    white wine
  115g/4oz/½ cup unsalted (sweet)
    butter, softened
  2–3 garlic cloves, finely chopped
  grated rind of 1 lemon
  60ml/4 tbsp finely chopped mixed
    herbs, such as parsley, chervil,
    tarragon and chives
  115g/4oz/1 cup fresh
    white breadcrumbs
  salt and ground black pepper
  lemon wedges, to serve

1 Check that all the mussels are closed after cleaning and discard any that remain open when sharply tapped.

2 Place the shallots and wine in a large pan and bring to the boil. Throw in the mussels and cover tightly. Cook over a high heat for 4–5 minutes, shaking the pan vigorously 2–3 times.

3 The mussels should be cooked and gaping open. Discard any that do not open after 5 minutes' cooking. Drain, reserving the cooking liquid.

4 Discard the top (empty) half of each shell. Place the mussels in a large roasting pan or heatproof dish.

5 Pour the cooking liquid into a clean pan and boil it vigorously until reduced to about 45ml/3 tbsp. Remove from the heat and leave to cool.

6 Cream the butter with the shallots from the reduced liquid, the garlic, lemon rind and herbs. Season well and chill until firm.

7 Distribute the flavoured butter among the mussels. Sprinkle with the cooking liquid, then sprinkle the breadcrumbs over the top.

8 Preheat the grill (broiler) and position the shelf about 10cm/4in below the heat. Grill (broil) the mussels until the butter is bubbling and the breadcrumbs are golden and crisp. Serve immediately, with wedges of lemon.

FLASH-FRIED SQUID <u>WITH</u> PAPRIKA <u>AND</u> GARLIC

THESE QUICK-FRIED SQUID ARE GOOD SERVED WITH A DRY SHERRY OR MANZANILLA AS AN APPETIZER OR AS PART OF MIXED TAPAS. ALTERNATIVELY, SERVE THEM ON A BED OF SALAD LEAVES AND OFFER WARM BREAD AS AN ACCOMPANIMENT FOR A MORE SUBSTANTIAL FIRST COURSE.

SERVES SIX TO EIGHT AS AN APPETIZER,
FOUR AS A FIRST COURSE

INGREDIENTS
   500g/1¼lb very small squid, cleaned
   90ml/6 tbsp olive oil, plus extra
   1 red chilli, seeded and
     finely chopped
   10ml/2 tsp Spanish mild smoked
     paprika (*pimentón*)
   30ml/2 tbsp plain (all-purpose) flour
   2 garlic cloves, finely chopped
   15ml/1 tbsp sherry vinegar
   5ml/1 tsp grated lemon rind
   30–45ml/2–3 tbsp finely chopped
     fresh parsley
salt and ground black pepper

1 Choose small squid that are no longer than 10cm/4in. Cut the body sacs into rings and cut the tentacles into bitesize pieces.

2 Place the squid in a bowl and add 30ml/2 tbsp of the oil, half the chilli and the paprika. Season with a little salt and some pepper, cover and marinate for 2–4 hours in the refrigerator.

COOK'S TIPS
• Make sure the wok or pan is very hot as the squid should cook for only 1–2 minutes: any longer and it will begin to toughen.
• Smoked paprika, known as *pimentón* in Spain, has a wonderful smoky flavour. If you cannot find it, use mild paprika.

3 Toss the squid in the flour and divide it into two batches. Heat the remaining oil in a preheated wok or deep frying pan over a high heat until very hot. Add the first batch of squid and stir-fry for 1–2 minutes, or until it becomes opaque and the tentacles have curled.

4 Sprinkle in half the garlic. Stir, then turn out on to a plate. Repeat with the second batch, adding more oil if needed.

5 Sprinkle over the sherry vinegar, lemon rind, remaining chilli and parsley. Season and serve hot or cool.

SALT COD FRITTERS WITH AIOLI

AIOLI IS A FIERCELY GARLICKY, OLIVE OIL MAYONNAISE FROM PROVENCE IN THE SOUTH OF FRANCE AND IS A TRADITIONAL ACCOMPANIMENT TO SALT COD.

SERVES SIX

INGREDIENTS
    450g/1lb salt cod
    500g/1¼lb floury potatoes
    300ml/½ pint/1¼ cups milk
    6 spring onions (scallions),
      finely chopped
    30ml/2 tbsp extra virgin olive oil
    30ml/2 tbsp chopped fresh parsley
    juice of ½ lemon, to taste
    2 eggs, beaten
    60ml/4 tbsp plain (all-purpose) flour
    90g/3½oz/1⅓ cups dry
      white breadcrumbs
    vegetable oil, for shallow frying
    salt and ground black pepper
    lemon wedges and salad, to serve
For the aioli
    2 large garlic cloves
    2 egg yolks
    300ml/½ pint/1¼ cups olive oil
    lemon juice, to taste

1 Soak the salt cod in cold water for 24–36 hours, changing the water five or six times. The cod should swell as it rehydrates and should not taste unpleasantly salty when tried. Drain.

2 Cook the potatoes, unpeeled, in a pan of boiling salted water for about 20 minutes, until tender. Drain, then peel and mash the potatoes.

3 Poach the cod very gently in the milk with half the spring onions for 10–15 minutes, or until it flakes easily. Remove the cod and flake it with a fork into a bowl, discarding bones and skin.

4 Add 60ml/4 tbsp mashed potato to the flaked cod and beat with a wooden spoon. Work in the olive oil, then gradually add the remaining potato. Beat in the remaining spring onions and the parsley. Season with lemon juice and pepper to taste – the mixture may need a little salt. Beat in one egg, then chill the mixture until firm.

5 Shape the mixture into 12–18 small round cakes. Coat them in flour, then dip them in the remaining egg and coat with the breadcrumbs. Chill until ready to fry.

COOK'S TIPS
• Try to find a thick, creamy white piece of salt cod, preferably cut from the middle of the fish rather than the tail and fin ends. Avoid thin, yellowish salt cod, as it will be too dry and salty.
• Mash potatoes by hand, never in a food processor, as it makes them gluey.
• Aioli traditionally has a sharp bite from the raw garlic. However, if you prefer a milder flavour, blanch the garlic once or twice in boiling water for about 3 minutes each time before using it.

6 Meanwhile, make the aioli. Place the garlic and a good pinch of salt in a mortar and pound to a paste with a pestle. Using a small whisk or a wooden spoon, gradually work in the egg yolks.

7 Add the olive oil, a drop at a time, until about half is incorporated. When the sauce is as thick as soft butter, beat in 5–10ml/1–2 tsp lemon juice, then continue adding oil until the aioli is very thick. Adjust the seasoning, adding lemon juice to taste.

8 Heat about 2cm/¾in depth of oil in a large, heavy frying pan. Add the fritters and cook over a medium-high heat for about 4 minutes. Turn them over and cook for a further 4 minutes on the other side, until crisp and golden. Drain thoroughly on crumpled kitchen paper, then serve with the aioli, lemon wedges and salad leaves.

ROASTED GARLIC AND GOAT'S CHEESE SOUFFLÉ

THE MELLOW FLAVOUR OF ROASTED GARLIC PERVADES THIS SIMPLE SOUFFLÉ. BALANCE THE RICH SOUFFLÉ WITH A CRISP GREEN SALAD, INCLUDING PEPPERY LEAVES, SUCH AS MIZUNA AND WATERCRESS.

5 Cook the sauce very gently for 10 minutes, stirring frequently. Season with salt, pepper and a pinch of cayenne. Cool slightly. Preheat the oven to 200°C/400°F/Gas 6.

6 Beat in the egg yolks one at a time. Then beat in the goat's cheese, all but 15ml/1 tbsp of the Parmesan and the chopped thyme. Use the remaining butter to grease one large soufflé dish (1 litre/1¾ pints/4 cups) or four large ramekins (about 250ml/8fl oz/1 cup).

7 Whisk the egg whites and cream of tartar in a scrupulously clean bowl until firm, but not dry. Stir 45ml/3 tbsp of the whites into the sauce, then gently, but thoroughly, fold in the remainder.

8 Pour the mixture into the prepared dish or dishes. Run a knife around the edge of each dish, pushing the mixture away from the rim. Sprinkle with the reserved Parmesan.

9 Place the dish or dishes on a baking sheet and cook for 25–30 minutes for a large soufflé or 20 minutes for small soufflés. The mixture should be risen and firm to a light touch in the centre; it should not wobble excessively when given a light push. Serve immediately.

SERVES THREE TO FOUR

INGREDIENTS
   2 large heads of garlic (choose heads
     with plump cloves)
   3 fresh thyme sprigs
   15ml/1 tbsp olive oil
   250ml/8fl oz/1 cup milk
   1 fresh bay leaf
   2 × 1cm/½in thick onion slices
   2 cloves
   50g/2oz/¼ cup butter
   40g/1½oz/⅓ cup plain (all-purpose)
     flour, sifted
   cayenne pepper
   3 eggs, separated, plus 1 egg white
   150g/5oz goat's cheese, crumbled
   50g/2oz/⅔ cup freshly grated
     Parmesan cheese
   5ml/1 tsp chopped fresh thyme
   2.5ml/½ tsp cream of tartar
   salt and ground black pepper

1 Preheat the oven to 180°C/350°F/ Gas 4. Place the garlic and thyme sprigs on a piece of foil. Sprinkle with the oil and close the foil around the garlic, then bake for about 1 hour, until the garlic is soft. Leave to cool.

2 Squeeze the garlic out of its skin. Discard the thyme and garlic skins, then purée the garlic flesh with the oil.

3 Meanwhile, place the milk, bay leaf, onion slices and cloves in a small pan. Bring to the boil, then remove from the heat. Cover and leave to stand for 30 minutes.

4 Melt 40g/1½oz/3 tbsp of the butter in another pan. Stir in the flour and cook gently for 2 minutes, stirring. Reheat and strain the milk, then gradually stir it into the flour and butter.

PASTA WITH GARLIC AND CHILLI

THIS IS THE SIMPLEST OF PASTA DISHES AND ONE OF THE BEST. MINT AND OREGANO GIVE VERY DIFFERENT RESULTS, BOTH GOOD. THERE IS NO NEED TO SERVE GRATED PARMESAN WITH THIS DISH — INSTEAD, LET THE CLEAR FLAVOUR OF THE GARLIC AND OLIVE OIL SING OUT.

SERVES THREE TO FOUR

INGREDIENTS
  400g/14oz dried spaghetti
  105ml/7 tbsp extra virgin olive oil,
    plus extra to taste
  1.5ml/¼ tsp dried red chilli flakes or
    2 small whole dried red chillies
  6 large garlic cloves, finely chopped
  15ml/1 tbsp chopped fresh mint
    or oregano
  15g/½ oz chopped fresh flat
    leaf parsley
  salt and ground black pepper

1 Cook the spaghetti in lightly salted, boiling water for 9–11 minutes, or according to the packet instructions, until just tender.

2 Meanwhile, warm the oil in a large frying pan or other suitable pan over a very gentle heat. Add the chilli flakes or whole chillies and cook very gently for 2–3 minutes.

COOK'S TIP
If you use fresh spaghetti, cook for only 2–3 minutes in salted, boiling water.

3 Add the garlic to the pan. Keep the heat very low, so that the garlic barely bubbles and does not brown, then cook, shaking the pan occasionally, for about 2 minutes. Remove the pan from the heat and cool a little, then add the fresh mint or oregano.

4 Drain the pasta, then immediately add it to the oil and garlic mixture, with the parsley. Toss thoroughly. Season with freshly ground black pepper and transfer to warmed serving bowls. Serve immediately, offering more olive oil at the table.

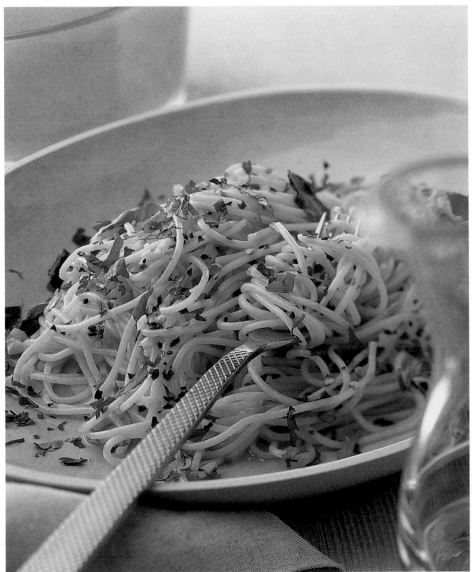

VARIATION
Cook 250g/9oz broccoli florets in boiling salted water for 4 minutes. Add to the chilli oil and gently fry for 5–8 minutes.

CHICKEN WITH FORTY CLOVES OF GARLIC

THIS DISH DOES NOT HAVE TO BE MATHEMATICALLY EXACT, SO DO NOT WORRY IF YOU HAVE 35 OR EVEN 50 CLOVES OF GARLIC — THE IMPORTANT THING IS THAT THERE SHOULD BE LOTS. THE SMELL THAT EMANATES FROM THE OVEN AS THE CHICKEN AND GARLIC COOK IS INDESCRIBABLY DELICIOUS.

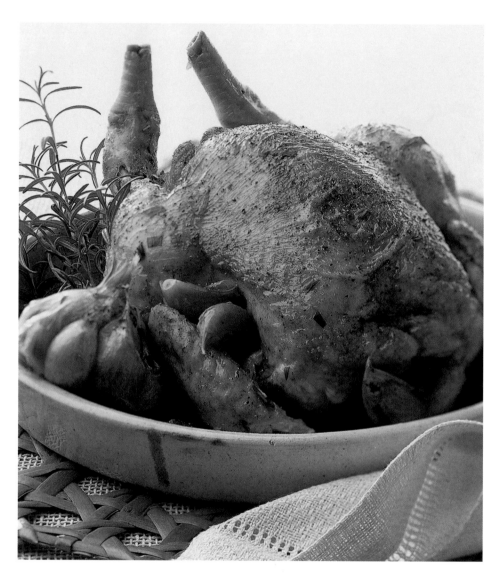

3 Sprinkle in 5ml/1 tsp flour and cook for 1 minute. Add the port or wine. Tuck in the whole heads of garlic and the peeled cloves with the herb sprigs. Pour over the remaining oil and season to taste with salt and pepper.

4 Mix the main batch of flour with sufficient water to make a firm dough. Roll it out into a long sausage and press it around the rim of the casserole, then press on the lid, folding the dough up and over it to create a tight seal. Cook in the oven for 1½ hours.

5 To serve, lift off the lid to break the seal and remove the chicken and whole garlic to a serving platter and keep warm. Remove and discard the herb sprigs, then place the casserole on the hob (stovetop) and whisk to combine the garlic cloves with the cooking juices. Add the crème fraîche, if using, and lemon juice to taste. Process the sauce in a food processor or blender or press through a sieve. Serve the garlic purée with the chicken.

SERVES FOUR TO FIVE

INGREDIENTS
5–6 whole heads of garlic
15g/½oz/1 tbsp butter
45ml/3 tbsp olive oil
1.8–2kg/4–4½lb chicken
150g/5oz/1¼ cups plain (all-purpose) flour, plus 5ml/1 tsp
75ml/5 tbsp white port, Pineau de Charentes or other white, fortified wine
2–3 fresh tarragon or rosemary sprigs
30ml/2 tbsp crème fraîche (optional)
few drops of lemon juice (optional)
salt and ground black pepper

1 Separate three of the heads of garlic into cloves and peel them. Remove the first layer of papery skin from the remaining heads of garlic and cut off the tops to expose the cloves, if you like, or leave them whole. Preheat the oven to 180°C/350°F/Gas 4.

2 Heat the butter and 15ml/1 tbsp of the olive oil in a flameproof casserole that is just large enough to take the chicken and garlic. Add the chicken and cook over a medium heat, turning frequently using two large forks, for 10–15 minutes, until it is golden brown all over.

GARLIC AND CHILLI MARINATED BEEF WITH CORN-CRUSTED ONION RINGS

FRUITY, SMOKY AND MILD MEXICAN CHILLIES COMBINE WELL WITH GARLIC IN THIS MARINADE FOR GRILLED STEAK. POLENTA MAKES A CRISP COATING FOR THE ACCOMPANYING FRIED ONION RINGS.

SERVES FOUR

INGREDIENTS

    20g/¾oz large mild dried red chillies
      (such as *mulato* or *pasilla*)
    2 garlic cloves, plain or smoked,
      finely chopped
    5ml/1 tsp ground toasted
      cumin seeds
    5ml/1 tsp dried oregano
    60ml/4 tbsp olive oil
    4 × 175–225g/6–8oz beef steaks:
      rump (round) or rib-eye
    salt and ground black pepper
For the onion rings
    2 onions, sliced into rings
    250ml/8fl oz/1 cup milk
    75g/3oz/¾ cup polenta or
      coarse corn meal
    2.5ml/½ tsp dried red
      chilli flakes
    5ml/1 tsp ground toasted
      cumin seeds
    5ml/1 tsp dried oregano
    vegetable oil, for deep-frying

3 Wash and dry the steaks, rub the chilli paste all over them and leave to marinate for up to 12 hours.

4 For the onion rings, soak the onions in the milk for 30 minutes. Mix the corn meal, chilli, cumin and oregano and season with salt and pepper.

5 Heat the oil for deep-frying to 160–180°C/325–350°F, or until a cube of day-old bread turns brown in about a minute.

6 Drain the onion rings and dip each one into the corn meal mixture, coating it thoroughly. Fry for 2–4 minutes, until browned and crisp. Do not overcrowd the pan, but cook in batches. Lift the onion rings out of the pan with a slotted spoon and drain on kitchen paper.

7 Heat a barbecue or cast-iron griddle pan. Season the steaks with salt and cook for about 4 minutes on each side for a medium result; reduce or increase this time according to how rare or well done you like steak. Serve the steaks with the onion rings.

1 Cut the stalks from the chillies and discard the seeds. Toast the chillies in a dry frying pan for 2–4 minutes, until they give off their aroma. Place the chillies in a bowl, cover with warm water and leave to soak for 20–30 minutes. Drain and reserve the water.

2 Process the chillies to a paste with the garlic, cumin, oregano and oil in a food processor. Add a little soaking water, if needed. Season with pepper.

FENNEL, POTATO AND GARLIC MASH

THIS FLAVOURSOME MASH OF POTATO, FENNEL AND GARLIC GOES PARTICULARLY WELL WITH FISH OR CHICKEN. IT IS ALSO EXTREMELY DELICIOUS WITH ROAST PORK.

SERVES FOUR

INGREDIENTS

1 head of garlic, separated
  into cloves
800g/1¾lb boiling potatoes, cut
  into chunks
2 large fennel bulbs
65g/2½oz/5 tbsp butter or 90ml/
  6 tbsp extra virgin olive oil
120–150ml/4–5fl oz/½–⅔ cup milk
  or single (light) cream
freshly grated nutmeg
salt and ground black pepper

1 If using a food mill to mash the potato, leave the garlic unpeeled, otherwise peel it. Boil the garlic with the potatoes in salted water for 20 minutes.

2 Meanwhile, trim and coarsely chop the fennel, reserving any feathery tops. Chop the tops and set them aside. Heat 25g/1oz/2 tbsp of the butter or 30ml/ 2 tbsp of the oil in a heavy pan. Add the fennel, cover and cook over a low heat for 20–30 minutes, until soft but not browned.

3 Drain and mash the potatoes and garlic. Purée the fennel in a food mill or blender and beat it into the potato with the remaining butter or olive oil.

COOK'S TIP

A food mill is good for mashing potatoes as it guarantees a smooth texture. Never mash potatoes in a food processor or blender as this releases the starch, giving a result that resembles wallpaper paste.

4 Warm the milk or cream and beat sufficient into the potato and fennel to make a creamy, light mixture. Season to taste and add a little grated nutmeg.

5 Reheat gently, then beat in any chopped fennel tops. Transfer to a warmed dish and serve immediately.

VARIATIONS

• For a stronger garlic flavour, use 30–45ml/2–3 tbsp roasted garlic purée.
• To give a stronger fennel flavour, cook 2.5–5ml/½–1 tsp ground fennel seeds with the fennel.
• For a slightly less rich mash, substitute hot stock for some or all of the milk or cream. Mash made with fish stock is particularly good with grilled (broiled) fish or as a topping for fish pie.

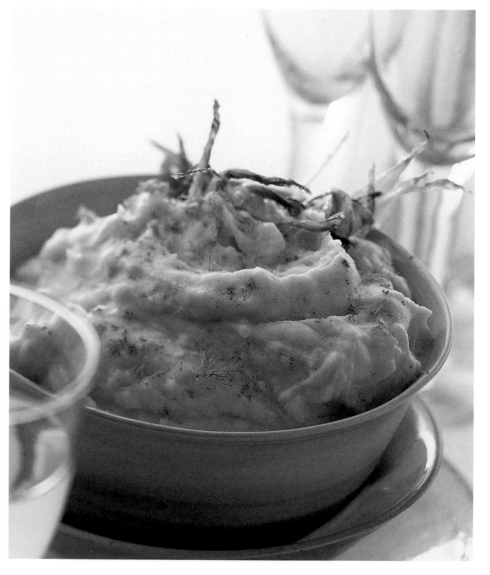

GARLIC AND HERB BREAD

EXCELLENT WITH SOUPS OR VEGETABLE FIRST COURSES, GARLIC BREAD IS ALSO IRRESISTIBLE JUST ON ITS OWN. THE BETTER THE BREAD, THE BETTER THE FINAL, BAKED VERSION WILL BE.

SERVES THREE TO FOUR

INGREDIENTS

1 baguette or bloomer loaf
For the garlic and herb butter
  115g/4oz/½ cup unsalted (sweet)
   butter, softened
  5–6 large garlic cloves, finely
   chopped or crushed
  30–45ml/2–3 tbsp chopped fresh
   herbs (such as parsley, chervil and
   a little tarragon)
  15ml/1 tbsp chopped fresh chives
  sea salt and ground black pepper

1 Preheat the oven to 200°C/400°F/ Gas 6. Make the garlic and herb butter by beating the butter with the garlic, herbs, chives and seasoning.

2 Cut the bread into 1cm/½in thick diagonal slices, but leave them attached at the base so that the loaf stays intact.

3 Spread the butter between the slices, being careful not to detach them, and spread any remaining butter over the top of the loaf.

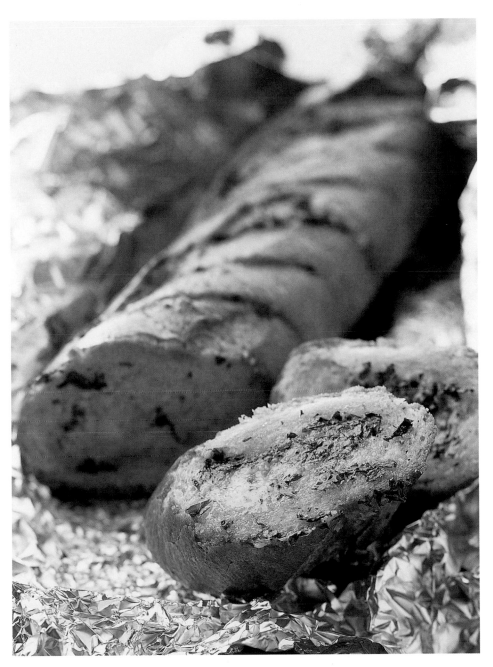

4 Wrap the loaf in foil and bake for 20–25 minutes, until the garlic and herb butter is melted and the crust is crisp. Cut into slices to serve.

VARIATIONS
• Use 105ml/7 tbsp extra virgin olive oil instead of butter.
• Flavour the butter with garlic, chopped fresh chilli, grated lime rind and chopped fresh coriander (cilantro).

• Add chopped, pitted black olives or sun-dried tomatoes to the butter with a little grated lemon rind.
• To make bruschetta, take thick slices of good country bread. Toast on a ridged cast-iron griddle pan, then rub with garlic and drizzle with extra virgin olive oil. For a stronger garlic taste, toast one side of the bread, spread some finely chopped garlic on the untoasted side, drizzle oil over, then toast until golden.

WALNUT AND GARLIC SAUCE

THIS SAUCE, SEVERAL VERSIONS OF WHICH CAN BE FOUND AROUND THE MEDITERRANEAN, IS EXCELLENT WITH ROAST OR POACHED CHICKEN OR STEAMED CAULIFLOWER OR POTATOES.

SERVES FOUR

INGREDIENTS
  2 × 1cm/½in slices good white bread, crusts removed
  60ml/4 tbsp milk
  150g/5oz/1¼ cups shelled walnuts
  4 garlic cloves, chopped
  120ml/4fl oz/½ cup mild olive oil
  15–30ml/1–2 tbsp walnut oil (optional)
  juice of 1 lemon
  salt and ground black pepper
  walnut or olive oil, for drizzling
  paprika, for dusting (optional)

VARIATION

For an Italian *salsa di noci* for pasta, process 90g/3½oz/scant 1 cup walnuts with 2 garlic cloves and 15g/½oz/½ cup flat leaf parsley. Blend in 1 slice white bread (crusts removed), soaked in milk, and 120ml/4fl oz/½ cup fruity olive oil as above. Season with salt, pepper and lemon juice. Thin with more milk or single (light) cream if very thick.

1 Soak the slices of white bread in the milk for about 5 minutes, then process with the walnuts and chopped garlic in a food processor or blender, to make a coarse paste.

2 Gradually add the olive oil to the paste with the motor still running, until the mixture forms a smooth thick sauce. Blend in the walnut oil, if using.

3 Scoop the sauce into a bowl and squeeze in lemon juice to taste, season with salt and pepper and beat well.

4 Transfer to a serving bowl, drizzle over a little more walnut or olive oil, then dust lightly with paprika, if using.

COOK'S TIP
Once opened, walnut oil has a fairly short shelf life. Buy it in small bottles and keep it in a cool, dark place. It is delicious in many salad dressings.

SALSA VERDE

THIS SIMPLE ITALIAN SAUCE IS A PURÉE OF FRESH HERBS WITH OLIVE OIL AND FLAVOURINGS. IT IS GOOD WITH POACHED OR ROAST BEEF AND CHICKEN, GRILLED STEAK OR GRILLED POLENTA.

SERVES FOUR

INGREDIENTS
  1–2 garlic cloves, finely chopped
  25g/1oz/1 cup flat leaf parsley leaves
  15g/½oz fresh coriander (cilantro), basil or mint or a mixture of herbs
  15ml/1 tbsp chopped chives
  15ml/1 tbsp salted capers, rinsed
  5 anchovy fillets in olive oil, drained and rinsed
  10ml/2 tsp French mustard (tarragon or *fines herbes* mustard are both good)
  120ml/4fl oz/½ cup extra virgin olive oil
  a little grated lemon rind and juice (optional)
  ground black pepper

1 Process the garlic, parsley, coriander, basil or mint, chives, capers, anchovies, mustard and 15ml/1 tbsp of the oil in a blender or food processor.

2 Gradually add the remaining oil in a thin stream with the motor running.

3 Transfer to a bowl and adjust the seasoning to taste – there should be enough salt from the capers and anchovies. Add a little lemon juice and rind if you like (especially if serving with fish). Serve immediately.

VARIATIONS
• Whisk in 30–45ml/2–3 tbsp crème fraîche to make a mild sauce that goes well with grilled (broiled) polenta, cauliflower and potatoes.
• Substitute fresh chervil, tarragon, dill or fennel – or a mixture of aniseed-flavoured herbs – for the coriander (cilantro), basil or mint to make a sauce that goes particularly well with poached or baked fish. It is also good with prawns (shrimp) and langoustines.

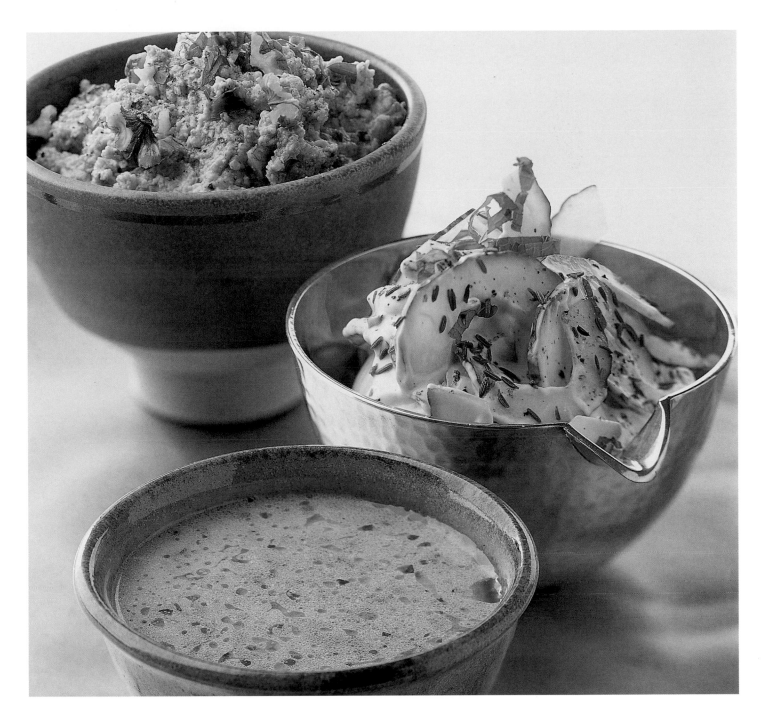

YOGURT WITH GARLIC, CUCUMBER AND MINT

VERSIONS OF THIS COOL, MINTY RELISH ARE FOUND IN GREECE (TZATZIKI), TURKEY (CACIK) AND THROUGHOUT THE MIDDLE EAST. IN INDIA, THE EQUIVALENT IS CALLED RAITA.

SERVES FOUR

INGREDIENTS
15cm/6in piece cucumber
5ml/1 tsp sea salt
300ml/½ pint/1¼ cups Greek
  (US strained plain) yogurt
3–4 garlic cloves, crushed
45ml/3 tbsp chopped fresh mint
ground black pepper
chopped fresh mint and/or ground
  toasted cumin seeds, to garnish

1 Slice, chop or grate the cucumber, then place it in a sieve and sprinkle with half the salt. Place the sieve on a deep plate and set aside for 30 minutes to drip.

2 Rinse the cucumber in cold water, pat dry and mix with the yogurt, garlic and mint. Season with salt and pepper. Leave for 30 minutes, then stir and sprinkle with fresh mint and/or toasted cumin to garnish.

VARIATION
To make a yogurt and garlic salad dressing, omit the cucumber and use 150ml/¼ pint/⅔ cup Greek (US strained plain) yogurt instead. Beat in 1 very finely chopped garlic clove, 5ml/1 tsp French mustard, salt and freshly ground black pepper to taste and a pinch of sugar. Finally, beat in 15–30ml/1–2 tbsp extra virgin olive oil and 15–30ml/ 1–2 tbsp chopped fresh herbs, such as mint, tarragon and chives, to taste.

Far from being the "poor relations", shallots, spring

onions (scallions) and chives are as lively and versatile as

any member of the Allium family. There is a lot more to

them than extra flavouring for salads, although you might

still like to try Salad of Roasted Shallots and Butternut

Squash with Feta Cheese, with recipes for soups, fritters,

skewers, dressings and a mouth-watering Spring Onion,

Chive and Ricotta Bread.

Cooking with Other Alliums

MISO BROTH WITH SPRING ONIONS AND TOFU

THE JAPANESE EAT MISO BROTH, A SIMPLE BUT HIGHLY NUTRITIOUS SOUP, ALMOST EVERY DAY — IT IS STANDARD BREAKFAST FARE AND IT IS EATEN WITH RICE OR NOODLES LATER IN THE DAY.

<u>SERVES FOUR</u>

INGREDIENTS
    1 bunch of spring onions (scallions)
      or 5 baby leeks
    15g/½oz fresh coriander (cilantro)
    3 thin slices fresh root ginger
    2 star anise
    1 small dried red chilli
    1.2 litres/2 pints/5 cups dashi stock
      or vegetable stock
    225g/8oz pak choi (bok choy) or
      other Asian greens, thickly sliced
    200g/7oz firm tofu, cut into
      2.5cm/1in cubes
    60ml/4 tbsp red miso
    30–45ml/2–3 tbsp Japanese soy
      sauce (shoyu)
    1 fresh red chilli, seeded and
      shredded (optional)

1 Cut the coarse green tops off the spring onions or baby leeks and slice the rest of the spring onions or leeks finely on the diagonal. Place the coarse green tops in a large pan with the coriander stalks, fresh root ginger, star anise, dried red chilli and dashi or vegetable stock.

2 Heat the mixture gently until boiling, then lower the heat and simmer for 10 minutes. Strain, return to the pan and reheat until simmering. Add the green portion of the sliced spring onions or leeks to the soup with the pak choi or greens and tofu. Cook for 2 minutes.

3 Mix 45ml/3 tbsp of the miso with a little of the hot soup in a bowl, then stir it into the soup. Taste the soup and add more miso with soy sauce to taste.

4 Coarsely chop the coriander leaves and stir most of them into the soup with the white part of the spring onions or leeks. Cook for 1 minute, then ladle the soup into warmed serving bowls. Sprinkle with the remaining coriander and the fresh red chilli, if using, and serve immediately.

COOK'S TIP
Dashi powder is available in most Asian and Chinese stores. Alternatively, make your own by gently simmering 10–15cm/4–6in kombu seaweed in 1.2 litres/2 pints/5 cups water for 10 minutes. Do not boil the stock vigorously, as this makes the dashi bitter. Remove the kombu, then add 15g/½oz dried bonito flakes and bring to the boil. Strain immediately through a fine sieve.

COCONUT AND SHELLFISH SOUP WITH GARLIC CHIVES

THE LONG LIST OF INGREDIENTS IN THIS THAI-INSPIRED RECIPE COULD MISLEAD YOU INTO THINKING THAT THIS SOUP IS COMPLICATED. IN FACT, IT IS VERY EASY TO PUT TOGETHER.

SERVES FOUR

INGREDIENTS
600ml/1 pint/2½ cups
  fish stock
5 thin slices fresh galangal or
  fresh root ginger
2 lemon grass stalks, chopped
3 kaffir lime leaves, shredded
25g/1oz garlic chives (1 bunch)
15g/½oz/½ cup fresh
  coriander (cilantro)
15ml/1 tbsp vegetable oil
4 shallots, chopped
400ml/14fl oz can coconut milk
30–45ml/2–3 tbsp Thai fish sauce
45–60ml/3–4 tbsp Thai green
  curry paste
450g/1lb raw large prawns (jumbo
  shrimp), peeled and deveined
450g/1lb prepared squid
a little lime juice (optional)
salt and ground black pepper
60ml/4 tbsp crisp-fried shallot
  slices, to serve

1 Pour the fish stock into a pan and add the slices of galangal or ginger, the lemon grass and half the shredded kaffir lime leaves.

2 Reserve a few garlic chives for the garnish, then chop the remainder. Add half the chopped garlic chives to the pan with the coriander stalks. Bring to the boil, reduce the heat and cover the pan, then simmer gently for 20 minutes. Strain the stock.

3 Rinse the pan. Add the oil and shallots. Cook over a medium heat for 5–10 minutes, until the shallots are just beginning to brown.

4 Stir in the strained stock, coconut milk, the remaining kaffir lime leaves and 30ml/2 tbsp of the fish sauce. Heat gently until simmering and cook over a low heat for 5–10 minutes.

VARIATIONS
• Instead of squid, you could add 400g/14oz firm white fish, such as monkfish, cut into small pieces.
• You could also replace the squid with mussels. Steam 675g/1½lb closed live mussels in a tightly covered pan for 3–4 minutes, or until the shells have opened. Discard any that remain shut, then remove the mussels from their shells.

5 Stir in the curry paste and prawns, then cook for 3 minutes. Add the squid and cook for a further 2 minutes. Add the lime juice, if using, and season, adding more fish sauce to taste.

6 Stir in the remaining chives and the coriander. Serve in bowls sprinkled with fried shallots and whole garlic chives.

Seafood and Spring Onion Skewers with Tartare Sauce

IF YOU MAKE THESE SKEWERS QUITE SMALL, THEY ARE GOOD AS A CANAPÉ TO SERVE AT A DRINKS PARTY OR BEFORE DINNER, WITH THE TARTARE SAUCE OFFERED AS A DIP.

MAKES NINE

INGREDIENTS
  675g/1½lb monkfish tail, filleted, skinned and membrane removed
  1 bunch spring onions (scallions)
  75ml/5 tbsp olive oil
  1 garlic clove, finely chopped
  15ml/1 tbsp lemon juice
  5ml/1 tsp dried oregano
  30ml/2 tbsp chopped fresh flat leaf parsley
  12–18 small scallops or large raw prawns (shrimp)
  75g/3oz/1½ cups fine fresh breadcrumbs
  salt and ground black pepper
For the tartare sauce
  2 egg yolks
  300ml/½ pint/1¼ cups olive oil, or vegetable oil and olive oil mixed
  15–30ml/1–2 tbsp lemon juice
  5ml/1 tsp French mustard, preferably tarragon mustard
  15ml/1 tbsp chopped gherkin or pickled cucumber
  15ml/1 tbsp chopped capers
  30ml/2 tbsp chopped fresh flat leaf parsley
  30ml/2 tbsp chopped fresh chives
  5ml/1 tsp chopped fresh tarragon

2 Whisk in 15ml/1 tbsp lemon juice, then a little more oil. Stir in all the mustard, gherkin or cucumber, capers, parsley, chives and tarragon. Add more lemon juice and seasoning to taste.

4 Mix the breadcrumbs and remaining parsley together. Toss the fish and spring onions in the mixture to coat. Soak nine skewers in cold water.

1 First make the tartare sauce. Whisk the egg yolks with a pinch of salt, then whisk in the oil, a drop at a time. When about half the oil is incorporated, add it in a thin stream, whisking constantly. Stop when the mayonnaise is very thick.

3 Cut the monkfish into 18 pieces and cut the spring onions into 18 pieces about 5–6cm/2–2½in long. Mix the oil, garlic, lemon juice, oregano and half the parsley with seasoning. Add the monkfish, scallops or prawns and spring onions, then marinate for 15 minutes.

5 Preheat the grill (broiler). Drain the skewers and thread the monkfish, scallops or prawns and spring onions on to them. Drizzle with a little marinade then grill (broil) for 5–6 minutes in total, turning once and drizzling with the marinade, until the fish is just cooked. Serve immediately with the sauce.

SPRING ONION AND RICOTTA FRITTERS WITH AVOCADO SALSA

THE FRESH-FLAVOURED SALSA SPIKED WITH A LITTLE RED ONION AND CHILLI IS EXCELLENT WITH THESE MELT-IN-THE-MOUTH HERBY SPRING ONION FRITTERS.

SERVES FOUR TO SIX

INGREDIENTS
    250g/9oz/generous 1 cup
      ricotta cheese
    1 large (US extra large) egg, beaten
    90ml/6 tbsp self-raising (self-
      rising) flour
    90ml/6 tbsp milk
    1 bunch spring onions (scallions),
      thinly sliced
    30ml/2 tbsp chopped fresh coriander
      (cilantro), plus extra to garnish
    sunflower oil, for shallow frying
    salt and ground black pepper
    lime wedges, to garnish
    200ml/7fl oz/scant 1 cup crème
      fraîche, to serve
For the salsa
    2 ripe, but not soft, avocados
    1 small red onion, diced
    grated rind and juice of 1 lime
    ½–1 fresh green or red chilli, seeded
      and finely chopped
    225g/8oz tomatoes, peeled, seeded
      and diced
    30–45ml/2–3 tbsp chopped mixed
      fresh mint and coriander (cilantro)
    pinch of caster (superfine) sugar
    5–10ml/1–2 tsp Thai fish sauce

2 Beat the ricotta until smooth, then beat in the egg and flour, followed by the milk to make a smooth, thick batter. Beat in the spring onions and coriander. Season well with pepper and a little salt.

3 Heat a little oil in a non-stick frying pan over a medium heat. Add spoonfuls of the mixture to make fritters about 7.5cm/3in across and fry for about 4–5 minutes each side, until set and browned. The mixture makes 12 fritters.

4 Taste the salsa and adjust the seasoning, adding more lime juice and/or sugar to taste. Serve the fritters immediately, with the salsa and a spoon of crème fraîche. Garnish with coriander and lime wedges.

VARIATION
The fritters are also good served with thinly sliced smoked salmon.

1 Make the salsa first. Peel, stone (pit) and dice the avocados. Place in a bowl with the red onion, lime rind and juice. Add chilli to taste, the tomatoes, mint and coriander. Season with salt, pepper, sugar and Thai fish sauce. Mix well and set aside for 30 minutes.

Deep-Fried Spring Onions <u>in</u> Beer Batter <u>with</u> Romesco Sauce

THIS PIQUANT, BUT NOT HOT, SAUCE FROM TARRAGONA IN SPAIN ADMIRABLY CUTS THE RICHNESS OF DEEP-FRIED FOOD, AND IT IS EXCELLENT WITH DEEP-FRIED SPRING ONIONS IN THEIR CRISP BATTER.

SERVES SIX

INGREDIENTS
    3 bunches plump spring onions
        (scallions), 18–24 in all
    sea salt and ground black pepper
    lemon wedges, to serve
For the batter
    225g/8oz/2 cups self-raising (self-
        rising) flour
    150ml/¼ pint/⅔ cup lager
    175–200ml/6–7fl oz/¾–scant 1 cup
        ice-cold water
    groundnut (peanut) oil, for
        deep-frying
    1 large (US extra large) egg white
    2.5ml/½ tsp cream of tartar
For the sauce
    2–3 large mild dried red chillies
    1 red (bell) pepper, halved and seeded
    2 large tomatoes, halved and seeded
    4–6 large garlic cloves, unpeeled
    75–90ml/5–6 tbsp olive oil
    25g/1oz/¼ cup hazelnuts, blanched
    4 slices French bread, each about
        2cm/¾in thick
    15ml/1 tbsp sherry vinegar
    squeeze of lemon juice (optional)
    chopped fresh parsley, to garnish

1 First prepare the sauce. Soak the dried chillies in hot water for about 30 minutes. Preheat the oven to 220°C/425°F/Gas 7.

2 Place the pepper halves, tomatoes and garlic on a baking sheet and drizzle with 15ml/1 tbsp olive oil.

3 Roast, uncovered, for about 30–40 minutes, until the pepper is blistered and blackened and the garlic is soft. Cool slightly, then peel the pepper, tomatoes and garlic.

4 Heat the remaining oil in a small frying pan and fry the hazelnuts until lightly browned, then transfer them to a plate. Fry the bread in the same oil until light brown on both sides, then transfer to the plate with the nuts and leave to cool. Reserve the oil from cooking.

5 Drain the chillies, discard as many of their seeds as you can, then place them in a food processor. Add the pepper, tomatoes, garlic, hazelnuts and bread with the reserved oil. Add the vinegar and process to a paste. Check the seasoning and thin the sauce with a little more oil or lemon juice, if necessary. Set aside.

6 Trim the roots from the spring onions. Trim the leaves to leave the onions about 15–18cm/6–7in long.

7 To make the batter, sift the flour into a bowl and add a good pinch each of salt and black pepper. Make a well in the centre, then gradually whisk in the lager, followed by the water. The batter should be the consistency of thick cream, so adjust the volume of water to produce this consistency.

8 Heat the oil for deep-frying to 180°C/350°F or until a cube of day-old bread browns in 30–45 seconds. Whisk the egg white with the cream of tartar until stiff, then fold it into the batter.

9 Dip the spring onions individually in the batter, drain off the excess and fry them in batches for 4–5 minutes. Drain thoroughly on kitchen paper and sprinkle with a little sea salt. Keep each batch warm until the next is cooked. Garnish with a little chopped parsley and serve hot with the sauce and lemon wedges.

Salad of Roasted Shallots and Butternut Squash with Feta Cheese

This is especially good served with a grain or starchy salad, based on rice or couscous, for example. Serve plenty of good bread to mop up the juices.

SERVES FOUR TO SIX

INGREDIENTS

   75ml/5 tbsp olive oil
   15ml/1 tbsp balsamic vinegar, plus a
     little extra if you like
   15ml/1 tbsp sweet soy sauce
   350g/12oz shallots, peeled but
     left whole
   3 fresh red chillies
   1 butternut squash, peeled, seeded
     and cut into chunks
   5ml/1 tsp finely chopped fresh thyme
   15g/½oz/½ cup flat leaf parsley
   1 small garlic clove, finely chopped
   75g/3oz/¾ cup walnuts, chopped
   150g/5oz feta cheese
   salt and ground black pepper

1 Preheat the oven to 200°C/400°F/
Gas 6. Beat the oil, vinegar and soy
sauce together in a large bowl, then
season with salt and pepper.

2 Toss the shallots and two chillies in
the oil mixture and turn into a large
roasting pan or ovenproof dish. Roast
for 15 minutes, stirring once or twice.

3 Add the butternut squash and roast
for a further 30–35 minutes, stirring
once, until the squash is tender and
browned. Remove from the oven, stir in
the chopped thyme and set the
vegetables aside to cool.

4 Chop the parsley and garlic together
and mix with the walnuts. Seed and
finely chop the remaining chilli.

5 Stir the parsley, garlic and walnut
mixture into the vegetables. Add
chopped chilli to taste and adjust the
seasoning, adding a little extra balsamic
vinegar if you like. Crumble the feta and
add to the salad. Transfer to a serving
dish and serve immediately.

POTATO AND MUSSEL SALAD WITH SHALLOT AND CHIVE DRESSING

SHALLOT AND CHIVES IN A CREAMY DRESSING ADD BITE TO THIS SALAD OF POTATO AND SWEET MUSSELS. SERVE WITH A BOWL OF FULL-FLAVOURED WATERCRESS AND PLENTY OF CRUSTY BREAD.

SERVES FOUR

INGREDIENTS
  675g/1½lb salad potatoes
  1kg/2¼lb mussels, scrubbed and
    beards removed
  200ml/7fl oz/ scant 1 cup dry
    white wine
  15g/½oz/½ cup fresh parsley, chopped
  salt and ground black pepper
  chopped fresh chives, to garnish
  watercress sprigs, to serve
For the dressing
  105ml/7 tbsp mild olive oil
  15–30ml/1–2 tbsp white wine vinegar
  5ml/1 tsp Dijon mustard
  1 large shallot, very finely chopped
  15ml/1 tbsp chopped fresh chives
  45ml/3 tbsp double (heavy) cream
  pinch of caster (superfine) sugar

1 Cook the potatoes in salted, boiling water for 15–20 minutes, or until tender. Drain, cool, then peel. Slice the potatoes into a bowl and toss with 30ml/2 tbsp of the oil for the dressing.

2 Discard any open mussels that do not close when sharply tapped and any with damaged shells. Bring the white wine to the boil in a large, heavy pan. Add the mussels, cover and boil vigorously, shaking the pan occasionally, for 3–4 minutes, until the mussels have opened. Discard any mussels that have not opened after 5 minutes' cooking. Drain and shell the mussels, reserving the cooking liquid.

3 Boil the reserved cooking liquid until reduced to about 45ml/3 tbsp. Strain this through a fine sieve over the potatoes and toss to mix.

4 For the dressing, whisk together the remaining oil, 15ml/1 tbsp vinegar, the mustard, shallot and chives.

5 Add the cream and whisk again to form a thick dressing. Adjust the seasoning, adding more vinegar and a pinch of sugar to taste.

6 Toss the mussels with the potatoes, then mix in the dressing and chopped parsley. Sprinkle with extra chopped chives and serve with watercress sprigs.

COOK'S TIP
Potato salads, such as this one, should not be chilled if at all possible, as the cold alters the texture of the potatoes and of the creamy dressing. For the best flavour and texture, serve this salad just cool or at room temperature.

SEARED SCALLOPS WITH CHIVE SAUCE ON LEEK AND CARROT RICE

SCALLOPS ARE ONE OF THE MOST DELICIOUS SHELLFISH. HERE THEY ARE PARTNERED WITH A DELICATE CHIVE SAUCE AND A PILAFF OF WILD AND WHITE RICE WITH SWEET LEEKS AND CARROTS.

SERVES FOUR

INGREDIENTS
    12–16 shelled scallops
    45ml/3 tbsp olive oil
    50g/2oz/⅓ cup wild rice
    65g/2½ oz/5 tbsp butter
    4 carrots, cut into long thin strips
    2 leeks, cut into thick,
      diagonal slices
    1 small onion, finely chopped
    115g/4oz/⅔ cup long grain rice
    1 fresh bay leaf
    200ml/7fl oz/scant 1 cup white wine
    450ml/¾ pint/scant 2 cups fish stock
    60ml/4 tbsp double (heavy) cream
    a little lemon juice
    25ml/5 tsp chopped fresh chives
    30ml/2 tbsp chervil sprigs
    salt and ground black pepper

1 Lightly season the scallops, brush with 15ml/1 tbsp of the olive oil and set aside.

2 Cook the wild rice in plenty of boiling water for about 30 minutes, until tender, then drain.

3 Melt half the butter in a small frying pan and cook the carrots fairly gently for 4–5 minutes. Add the leeks and cook for another 2 minutes. Season with salt and pepper and add 30–45ml/ 2–3 tbsp water, then cover and cook for a few minutes more. Uncover and cook until the liquid has reduced. Set aside off the heat.

4 Melt half the rest of the butter with 15ml/1 tbsp of the remaining oil in a heavy pan. Add the onion and cook gently for 3–4 minutes, until softened but not browned.

5 Add the long grain rice and bay leaf and cook, stirring constantly, until the rice looks translucent and the grains are coated with oil.

6 Pour in half the wine and half the stock. Season with 2.5ml/½ tsp salt and bring to the boil. Stir, then cover and cook very gently for 15 minutes, or until the liquid is absorbed and the rice is cooked and tender.

7 Reheat the carrots and leeks gently, then stir them into the long grain rice with the wild rice. Add seasoning to taste, if necessary.

8 Meanwhile, pour the remaining wine and stock into a small pan and boil rapidly until reduced by half.

COOK'S TIP
Choose fresh, rather than frozen, scallops as the frozen ones tend to exude water on cooking. Scallops need only the briefest cooking at high heat, just until they turn opaque and brown on each side, so have the pan very hot. Although some people avoid eating the orange-coloured coral, it is delicious and many people consider it to be the best bit.

9 Heat a heavy frying pan over a high heat. Add the remaining butter and oil. Sear the scallops for 1–2 minutes each side, then set aside and keep warm.

10 Pour the reduced stock into the pan and heat until bubbling, then add the cream and boil until thickened. Season with lemon juice, salt and pepper. Stir in the chives and scallops.

11 Stir the chervil into the rice and pile it on to plates. Arrange the scallops on top and spoon the sauce over the rice.

CHICKEN BAKED WITH SHALLOTS AND FENNEL

THIS IS A VERY SIMPLE AND DELICIOUS WAY TO COOK CHICKEN. IF YOU HAVE TIME, LEAVE THE CHICKEN TO MARINATE FOR A FEW HOURS FOR THE BEST FLAVOUR.

SERVES FOUR

INGREDIENTS

1.6–1.8kg/3½–4lb chicken pieces
250g/9oz shallots, peeled
1 head garlic, separated into cloves
  and peeled
60ml/4 tbsp extra virgin olive oil
45ml/3 tbsp tarragon vinegar
45ml/3 tbsp white wine or
  vermouth (optional)
5ml/1 tsp fennel seeds, crushed
2 bulbs fennel, cut into wedges,
  feathery tops reserved
150ml/¼ pint/⅔ cup double
  (heavy) cream
5ml/1 tsp redcurrant jelly
15ml/1 tbsp tarragon mustard
caster (superfine) sugar (optional)
30ml/2 tbsp chopped fresh flat
  leaf parsley
salt and ground black pepper

1 Place the chicken pieces, shallots and all but one of the garlic cloves in a flameproof dish or roasting pan. Add the oil, vinegar, wine or vermouth, if using, and fennel seeds. Season with pepper, then marinate for 2–3 hours.

2 Preheat the oven to 190°C/375°F/ Gas 5. Add the fennel to the chicken, season with salt and stir to mix.

3 Cook the chicken in the oven for 50–60 minutes, stirring once or twice. The chicken juices should run clear, not pink, when the thick thigh meat is pierced with a skewer.

4 Transfer the chicken and vegetables to a serving dish and keep them warm. Skim off some of the fat and bring the cooking juices to the boil, then pour in the cream. Stir, scraping up all the delicious juices. Whisk in the redcurrant jelly, followed by the tarragon mustard. Check the seasoning, adding a little sugar if you like.

5 Chop the remaining garlic with the fennel tops and mix with the parsley. Pour the sauce over the chicken and sprinkle the chopped garlic and herb mixture over the top. Serve immediately.

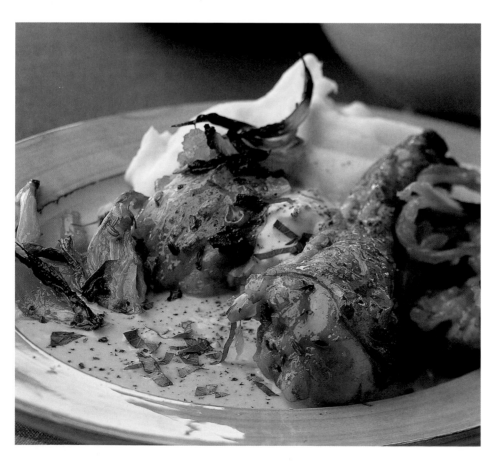

COOK'S TIPS
• If possible, use the fresh new season's garlic for this dish, as it is plump, moist and full of flavour. Purple-skinned garlic is considered by many cooks to have the best flavour.
• The cut surfaces of fennel quickly discolour, so do not prepare it much in advance of using it. If you must prepare it beforehand, then put the wedges into a bowl of cold water acidulated with a little lemon juice.

STIR-FRIED BEEF AND MUSHROOMS WITH BLACK BEANS AND SPRING ONIONS

THE COMBINATION OF GARLIC AND SALTED BLACK BEANS IS A CLASSIC CANTONESE SEASONING FOR BEEF. SERVE RICE AND SIMPLE BRAISED CHINESE GREENS AS ACCOMPANIMENTS.

SERVES FOUR

INGREDIENTS
30ml/2 tbsp soy sauce
30ml/2 tbsp Chinese rice wine or
   dry sherry
10ml/2 tsp cornflour (cornstarch)
10ml/2 tsp sesame oil
450g/1lb fillet or rump (round) steak,
   trimmed of fat
12 dried shiitake mushrooms
   (Chinese black mushrooms)
25ml/1½ tbsp salted black beans
5ml/1 tsp caster (superfine) sugar
120ml/4fl oz/½ cup groundnut
   (peanut) oil
4 garlic cloves, thinly sliced
2.5cm/1in piece fresh root ginger,
   cut into fine strips
200g/7oz open cap
   mushrooms, sliced
1 bunch spring onions (scallions),
   sliced diagonally
1 fresh red chilli, seeded and
   finely shredded
salt and ground black pepper

1 Mix half the soy sauce, half the rice wine or sherry, half the cornflour and all the sesame oil with 15ml/1 tbsp cold water until smooth. Add a good pinch of salt and pepper.

2 Cut the beef into very thin slices, no more than 5mm/¼in thick. Add the slices to the cornflour mixture and rub the mixture into the beef with your fingers. Set aside for 30 minutes.

3 Pour boiling water over the dried mushrooms and soak for 25 minutes. Drain, reserving 45ml/3 tbsp of the soaking water. Remove and discard the hard stalks and cut the caps in half.

4 Using a fork, mash the black beans with the caster sugar in a small bowl. Stir the remaining cornflour, soy sauce and rice wine or sherry together in another small bowl.

5 Heat the oil in a wok until very hot, then stir-fry the beef for 30–45 seconds, until just brown. Use a slotted spoon to transfer it to a plate. Pour off some oil to leave about 45ml/3 tbsp in the wok.

6 Add the garlic and ginger, stir-fry for 1 minute, then add the shiitake and fresh mushrooms and stir-fry for 2 minutes. Set aside a few tablespoons of the green part of the spring onions, then add the rest to the wok. Stir, add the mashed black beans and stir-fry for another 1–2 minutes.

7 Stir the beef back into the mixture in the wok, then add 45ml/3 tbsp of the shiitake soaking water. Let the mixture bubble. Stir the cornflour mixture to mix it well, pour it into the wok, stirring, and simmer until the sauce thickens. Sprinkle the chilli and reserved spring onions over the beef and serve.

GARLIC CHIVE RICE <u>WITH</u> MUSHROOMS

*RICE IS READILY INFUSED WITH THE PUNGENT AROMA AND FLAVOUR OF GARLIC CHIVES, CREATING
A DISH WITH AN EXCELLENT FLAVOUR. SERVE WITH VEGETARIAN DISHES, FISH OR CHICKEN.*

3 Add the rice to the onions and fry over a low heat, stirring frequently, for 4–5 minutes. Pour in the stock mixture, then stir in 5ml/1 tsp salt and a good grinding of black pepper. Bring to the boil, stir and reduce the heat to very low. Cover tightly and cook for 15–20 minutes, until the rice has absorbed all the liquid.

4 Lay a clean, folded dishtowel over the pan under the lid and press on the lid to wedge it firmly in place. Leave to stand for 10 minutes, allowing the towel to absorb the steam while the rice becomes completely tender.

5 Meanwhile, heat the remaining oil in a frying pan and cook the mushrooms for 5–6 minutes, until tender and browned. Add the remaining chives and cook for another 1–2 minutes.

6 Stir the mushrooms and chopped coriander leaves into the rice. Adjust the seasoning, transfer to a warmed serving dish and serve immediately, sprinkled with the cashew nuts.

SERVES FOUR

INGREDIENTS
   350g/12oz/generous 1½ cups
     long grain rice
   60ml/4 tbsp groundnut (peanut) oil
   1 small onion, finely chopped
   2 green chillies, seeded and
     finely chopped
   25g/1oz garlic chives, chopped
   15g/½oz/½ cup fresh
     coriander (cilantro)
   600ml/1 pint/2½ cups vegetable or
     mushroom stock
   5ml/1 tsp salt
   250g/9oz mixed mushrooms, sliced
   50g/2oz cashew nuts, fried in 15ml/
    1 tbsp oil until golden brown
   ground black pepper

1 Wash and drain the rice. Heat half the oil in a pan and cook the onion and chillies over a gentle heat, stirring occasionally, for 10–12 minutes, until soft but not browned.

2 Set half the garlic chives aside. Cut the stalks off the coriander and set the leaves aside. Purée the remaining chives and the coriander stalks with the stock in a blender or food processor.

COOK'S TIP
Wild mushrooms are often expensive, but they do have distinctive flavours. Mixing them with cultivated mushrooms is an economical way of using them. Look for oyster mushrooms, ceps, chanterelles, morels, and horse mushrooms.

SPRING ONION, CHIVE AND RICOTTA BREAD

RICOTTA CHEESE AND CHIVES MAKE A MOIST, WELL-FLAVOURED LOAF THAT IS EXCELLENT FOR SANDWICHES. SHAPE THE DOUGH INTO ROLLS, LOAVES, A COTTAGE LOAF, OR EVEN A PLAIT.

MAKES ONE LOAF OR SIXTEEN ROLLS

INGREDIENTS

15g/½oz fresh yeast or 10ml/2 tsp
   active dried yeast
5ml/1 tsp caster (superfine) sugar
270ml/9fl oz/generous 1 cup
   lukewarm water
450g/1lb unbleached strong white
   bread flour, plus a little extra
7.5ml/1½ tsp salt
1 large (US extra large) egg, beaten
115g/4oz/½ cup ricotta cheese
1 bunch spring onions (scallions),
   thinly sliced
30ml/2 tbsp extra virgin olive oil
45ml/3 tbsp chopped fresh chives
15ml/1 tbsp milk
10ml/2 tsp poppy seeds (optional)
coarse sea salt

1 Cream fresh yeast with the sugar and stir in 120ml/4fl oz/½ cup of the water. For dried yeast, stir the sugar into the water, then sprinkle it over the surface. Leave in a warm place for 10 minutes.

2 Sift the flour and salt into a warmed bowl. Make a well in the centre and pour in the yeast liquid and the remaining water. Save a little beaten egg, then put the rest in the bowl. Add the ricotta and mix to form a dough, adding a little more flour if the mixture is very sticky.

3 Knead the dough on a floured work surface until smooth and elastic. Set aside in a greased bowl, inside a plastic bag, in a warm place for 1–2 hours, until doubled in size.

4 Meanwhile, cook the spring onions in the oil for 3–4 minutes, until soft but not browned. Set aside to cool.

5 Knock back (punch down) the risen dough and knead in the spring onions, with their oil from cooking, and the chives. Shape the dough into rolls or a large or small loaf.

6 Grease a baking sheet or loaf tin (pan) and place the rolls or bread on it. Cover with greased plastic or oiled clear film (plastic wrap) and leave in a warm place to rise for about 1 hour. Preheat the oven to 200°C/400°F/Gas 6.

7 Beat the milk into the reserved beaten egg and use to glaze the rolls or loaf. Sprinkle with poppy seeds, if using, and a little coarse sea salt, then bake rolls for about 15 minutes or a loaf for 30–40 minutes or until golden and well risen. When tapped firmly on the base, the bread should feel and sound firm. Cool on a wire rack.

COOK'S TIP

To make a plait (braid), divide the dough into three sausage-shaped pieces about 40cm/16in long. Press them together at one end and then plait, pressing the ends together when completed.

INDEX

ACKNOWLEDGEMENTS

Photographs are all by William Lingwood except those on the following pages: p6, p7b, p18 The Anthony Blake Photo Library; p7t, p19b Cephas; p8, p13tr, p14t, p17b, p20 The Bridgeman Art Library; p9t, p10t, p10b The Ancient Egypt Picture Library; p9b, p10b, p11t, p11b, p13tl, p14b, p16t, p16b, p21t, p21b, p22b, p23t Mary Evans Picture Library; p12, p14b, p15 e.t. archive; p13b, p22t, p23b AKG Photographic Library; p17t Hulton Getty Picture Library; p19t Food Features; p24,

p28b John Freeman; p28r, p36l, A–Z Botanical Collection Ltd; p37tl Michelle Garrett.
  The author would like to acknowledge the following for their inspiration and information: John Ayto, A Gourmet's Guide (Oxford, 1994); Lindsey Bareham, Onions Without Tears (London, 1995); Barbara Ciletti, The Onion Harvest Cookbook (Newtown, CT, 1998); Bruce Cost, Foods from the Far East (London, 1990); William J. Darby and Paul Ghalioungui, Food: The Gift of Osiris, 2 volumes (London, 1977); Alan Davidson, The

Oxford Companion to Food (Oxford, 1999); John Edwards, The Roman Cookery of Apicius (London, 1984); John Evelyn, Acetaria: A Discourse of Sallets (1699), edited by Christopher Driver and Tom Jaine (Totnes, 1996); Four Seasons of the House of Cerruti, edited and translated by Judith Spencer (New York, NY, 1983); M. Grieve, A Modern Herbal, edited by C. F. Leyel (London, 1931, 1998); Dorothy Hartley, Food in England (1954, 1996); Katy Holder and Gail Duff, A Clove of Garlic (London, 1996);

C. F. Leyel and Olga Hartley, The Gentle Art of Cookery (London, 1925, 1974); Harold McGee, On Food and Cooking: The Science and Lore of the Kitchen (London, 1991); Charmaine Solomon, The Encyclopedia of Asian Food (London, 1998); Colin Spencer, Vegetable Book (London, 1995); Tom Stobart, The Cook's Encyclopaedia (London, 1998); Waverley Root, Food (New York, NY, 1980); J. G. Vaughan and C. A. Geissler, The New Oxford Book of Food Plants (Oxford, 1997).